THE MOST IMPORTANT
WORDS IN ENGLISH AND CHINESE

have been gathered together in one easy-to-use guide. From "able" to "zero," here are the 1,000 most useful and necessary words for proper communication between English- and Chinese-speaking people. Based on C. K. Ogden's list of the 850 most frequently used words in the English language, and on other studies on frequency of word usage, this handy dictionary insures that whatever your need, you'll always be able to find the words to express yourself in—

THE BASIC ENGLISH-CHINESE
CHINESE-ENGLISH DICTIONARY

THE BASIC
ENGLISH-
CHINESE
CHINESE-
ENGLISH
DICTIONARY

USING SIMPLIFIED CHARACTERS
(WITH AN APPENDIX CONTAINING THE
ORIGINAL COMPLEX CHARACTERS)

TRANSLITERATED IN
ACCORDANCE WITH THE NEW,
OFFICIAL CHINESE PHONETIC ALPHABET

Compiled by Peter M. Bergman

Joint Compilers:
Teruko Hayashi
Miyuko Hayashi
Yoko Nagano

A SIGNET BOOK

NEW AMERICAN LIBRARY

A DIVISION OF PENGUIN BOOKS USA INC.

Copyright © 1980 by Peter Bergman

All rights reserved. For information address Peter Bergman,
Bethlehem, Connecticut 06751.

This is an authorized reprint of a hardcover edition published
by the Polyglot Library.

Ø

SIGNET TRADEMARK REG. U.S. PAT. OFF. AND FOREIGN COUNTRIES
REGISTERED TRADEMARK—MARCA REGISTRADA
HECHO EN DRESDEN, TN, U.S.A.

SIGNET, SIGNET CLASSIC, MENTOR, ONYX, PLUME, MERIDIAN
and NAL BOOKS are published by New American Library, a division of
Penguin Books USA Inc., 1633 Broadway, New York, New York 10019

Library of Congress Cataloging in Publication Data
Bergman, Peter M.
The basic English-Chinese, Chinese-English dictionary.

(A Signet book)
1. English language—Dictionaries—Chinese.
2. Chinese language—Dictionaries—English.
I. Title.
[PL1455.B4   1980b]   495.1'321   80-352
ISBN 0-451-08262-7

First Signet Printing, June, 1980

6   7   8   9   10   11   12   13   14

PRINTED IN THE UNITED STATES OF AMERICA

Contents

Introductory Note

The purpose of this compact little book is to help the reader to communicate easily with Chinese-speaking people. Its uniqueness is the **numerical** order in which it is arranged. An Arabic number is attached to each word—always the same number for the respective word no matter in which section of the book it is found. English is alphabetized, while Chinese is indexed according to the number of strokes. The transliteration follows the official Romanization with the pronunciation accents for Mandarin.

The underlying idea is not to "computerize." It is that numbers are the only existent international "language" (to a certain degree musical notation also has this quality) used almost uniformly all over the world. This method is especially appropriate for the Chinese language which, with its highly complicated system of character strokes instead of an alphabet, is difficult even for linguists to master. Not knowing a single stroke of Chinese writing or the idiocyncrasies of the four-tone pronunciation (which practically only a native is able to grasp), one has simply to follow the number attached to the word and thereby find the meaning of the word with its approximate transliteration.

The book can be used with equal ease by any Chinese, although it is based on the official Mandarin language. Universality of the stroke signs and of the numbers attached to each word in this book makes this possible.

Limitation of the vocabulary to 1000 words follows the pioneering work of C. K. Ogden's "Basic English," with its 850 most frequently used words; additional selections were based on studies of word frequency computations, especially for travelers. One thousand words surpasses the vocabulary used by educated people in daily life.

English	Simplified Chinese	Pinyin (with tone-accents)	Romanized transliteration
1 able	能 1	néng 1	neng 1
2 abroad	国外 2	guó wài 2	gwo way 2
3 absent	缺席 3	quē xí 3	chiue shyi 3
4 accept	接受 4	jiē shòu 4	jie show 4
5 accident	事故 5	shì gù 5	shyh guh 5
6 accompany	陪伴 6	péi bàn 6	peir bann 6
7 account	算账 7	suàn zhàng 7	suann janq 7
8 across	横过 8	héng guò 8	herng guoh 8
9 address	地址 9	dì zhǐ 9	dih jyy 9
10 advice	劝告 10	quàn gào 10	chiuann gaw 10
11 affair	事件 11	shì jiàn 11	shyh jiann 11
12 after	以后 12	yǐ hòu 12	yii how 12
13 afternoon	下午 13	xià wǔ 13	shiah wuu 13
14 again	再 14	zài 14	tzay 14
15 against	对 15	duì 15	duey 15
16 age	年岁 16	nián suì 16	nian suey 16
17 agree	同意 17	tóng yì 17	torng yih 17
18 aim	目的 18	mù dì 18	muh dih 18
19 air	空气 19	kōng qì 19	kong chih 19
20 airplane	飞机 20	fēi jī 20	fei ji 20

English	Simplified Chinese	Pinyin (with tone-accents)	Romanized transliteration
21 airport	机场 21	jī chǎng 21	ji chaang 21
22 all	全部 22	quán bù 22	chyuan buh 22
23 all right	好 23	hǎo 23	hao 23
24 alone	独自 24	dú zì 24	dwu tzyh 24
25 already	已经 25	yǐjing 25	yii-jing 25
26 also	也 26	yě 26	yee 26
27 altitude	高度 27	gāo dù 27	gau duh 27
28 always	经常 28	jīng cháng 28	jing charng 28
29 and	和 29	hé 29	her 29
30 angry	生气 30	shēng qì 30	sheng chih 30
31 animal	动物 31	dòng wù 31	donq wuh 31
32 ankle	脚脖子 32	jiǎo bózi 32	jeau bortz 32
33 answer	回答 33	huí dá 33	hwei dar 33
34 ant	蚂蚁 34	mǎ yǐ 34	maa yii 34
35 apartment	公寓 35	gōng yù 35	gong yuh 35
36 appear	出现 36	chū xiàn 36	chu shiann 36
37 appetite	食欲 37	shí yù 37	shyr yuh 37
38 apple	苹果 38	píng guǒ 38	pyng guoo 38
39 appointment	约定 39	yuē dìng 39	iue dinq 39
40 apricot	杏 40	xìng 40	shinq 40

English	Simplified Chinese	Pinyin (with tone-accents)	Romanized transliteration
41 April	四月 41	sì yuè 41	syh yueh 41
42 arm	胳臂 42	gēbei 42	ge-bey 42
43 arrival	到达 43	dào dá 43	daw dar 43
44 art	艺术 44	yì shù 44	yih shuh 44
45 artificial	人造 45	rén zào 45	ren tzaw 45
46 ask	问 46	wèn 46	wenn 46
47 asparagus	芦笋 47	lú sǔn 47	lu soen 47
48 August	八月 48	bá yuè 48	bar yueh 48
49 aunt	姑母 49	gū mǔ 49	gu muu 49
50 authority	权威 50	quán wēi 50	chyuan uei 50
51 autumn	秋天 51	qiū tiān 51	chiou tian 51
52 available	有效 52	yǒu xiào 52	yeou shiaw 52
53 awaken	唤醒 53	huàn xǐng 53	huann shiing 53
54 baby	娃娃 54	wá wa 54	wa-wa 54
55 bachelor	单身汉 55	dān shēn hàn 55	dan shen hann 55
56 back	背脊 56	bèi jǐ 56	bey jii 56
57 backward	向后 57	xiàng hòu 57	shiang how 57
58 bad	坏 58	huài 58	huay 58
59 bag	包 59	bāo 59	bau 59
60 baggage	行李 60	xíng lǐ 60	shyng lii 60

English	Simplified Chinese	Pinyin (with tone-accents)	Romanized transliteration
61 bake	烘 61	hōng 61	hong 61
62 baker	面包师傅 62	miàn bāo shī fù 62	miann bau shy fuh 62
63 bald	秃 63	tū 63	tu 63
64 ball	球 64	qiú 64	chyou 64
65 bandage	绷带 65	bēng dài 65	beng day 65
66 bargain	廉价品 66	lián jià pǐn 66	lian jiah piin 66
67 barley	大麦 67	dà mài 67	dah may 67
68 barrel	桶 68	tǒng 68	toong 68
69 basement	地下室 69	dì xià shì 69	dih shiah shyh 69
70 bashful	怕羞 70	pà xiū 70	pah shiou 70
71 basket	篮子 71	lánzi 71	lantz 71
72 bath	洗澡 72	xǐ zǎo 72	shii tzao 72
73 bathrobe	浴衣 73	yù yī 73	yuh i 73
74 bathtub	澡盆 74	zǎo pén 74	tzao pern 74
75 be	是 75	shì 75	shyh 75
76 beach	海滩 76	hǎi tān 76	hae tan 76
77 bean	豆子 77	dòuzi 77	dowtz 77
78 bear	熊 78	xióng 78	shyong 78
79 beard	胡子 79	húzi 79	hwutz 79
80 beautiful	美丽 80	měi lì 80	meei lih 80

English	Simplified Chinese	Pinyin (with tone-accents)	Romanized transliteration
81 because	因为 81	yīn wèi 81	in wey 81
82 bed	床 82	chuáng 82	chwang 82
83 bedbug	臭虫 83	chòu chóng 83	chow chorng 83
84 bee	蜜蜂 84	mì fēng 84	mih feng 84
85 beef	牛肉 85	niú ròu 85	niou row 85
86 beer	啤酒 86	pí jiǔ 86	pyi jeou 86
87 beggar	乞丐 87	qǐ gài 87	chii gay 87
88 begin	开始 88	kāi shǐ 88	kai shyy 88
89 behavior	行为 89	xíng wéi 89	shyng wei 89
90 behind	在后 90	zài hòu 90	tzay how 90
91 believe	相信 91	xiāng xìn 91	shiang shinn 91
92 bell	铃子 92	língzi 92	lingtz 92
93 belly	肚子 93	dùzi 93	duhtz 93
94 below	在下 94	zài xià 94	tzay shiah 94
95 belt	腰带 95	yāo dài 95	iau day 95
96 berry	浆果 96	jiāng guǒ 96	jiang guoo 96
97 bet	打赌 97	dǎ dǔ 97	daa duu 97
98 betray	背叛 98	bèi pàn 98	bey pann 98
99 between	…之间 99	…zhī jiān 99	…jy jian 99
100 bicycle	自行车 100	zì xíng chē 100	tzyh shyng che 100

English	Simplified Chinese	Pinyin (with tone-accents)	Romanized transliteration
101 bill	账单 101	zhàng dān 101	janq dan 101
102 bird	鸟 102	niǎo 102	neau 102
103 birth	诞生 103	dàn shēng 103	dann sheng 103
104 birthday	生日 104	shēng rì 104	sheng ryh 104
105 bitter	苦 105	kǔ 105	kuu 105
106 black	黑 106	hēi 106	hei 106
107 bladder	膀胱 107	páng guāng 107	parng guang 107
108 blame	谴责 108	qiǎn zé 108	chean tzer 108
109 blanket	毛毯 109	máo tǎn 109	mau taan 109
110 bleach	漂白 110	piǎo bái 110	peau bair 110
111 blind	瞎 111	xiā 111	shia 111
112 blonde	金发 112	jīn fà 112	jin fa 112
113 blood	血 113	xuè 113	shiueh 113
114 blouse	衬衫 114	chèn shān 114	chenn shan 114
115 blue	蓝 115	lán 115	lan 115
116 boat	船 116	chuán 116	chwan 116
117 body	身体 117	shēn tǐ 117	shen tii 117
118 boil	烙 118	shāo 118	shau 118
119 bone	骨头 119	gútou 119	gwu-tou 119
120 book	书 120	shū 120	shu 120

English	Simplified Chinese	Pinyin (with tone-accents)	Romanized transliteration
121 border	边界 121	biān jiè 121	bian jieh 121
122 bottle	瓶子 122	píngzi 122	pyngtz 122
123 bowl	碗 123	wǎn 123	woan 123
124 boy	男孩子 124	nán háizi 124	nan hairtz 124
125 bracelet	手镯 125	shǒu zhuó 125	shoou jwo 125
126 brain	脑子 126	nǎozi 126	naotz 126
127 brake	制动器 127	zhì dòng qì 127	jyh donq chih 127
128 brass	黄铜 128	huáng tóng 128	hwang torng 128
129 bread	面包 129	miàn bāo 129	miann bau 129
130 breakfast	早饭 130	zǎo fàn 130	tzao fann 130
131 breast	胸脯 131	xiōng pú 131	shiong pwu 131
132 breath	气息 132	qì xī 132	chih shi 132
133 brick	砖 133	zhuān 133	juan 133
134 bride	新娘 134	xīn niáng 134	shin niang 134
135 bridge	桥 135	qiáo 135	chyau 135
136 bring	带来 136	dài lái 136	day lai 136
137 broom	扫帚 137	sàozhou 137	saw-joou 137
138 brother	弟兄 138	dì xiōng 138	dih shiong 138
139 brown	褐色 139	hè sè 139	heh seh 139
140 brush	刷子 140	shuāzi 140	shuatz 140

English	Simplified Chinese	Pinyin (with tone-accents)	Romanized transliteration
141 building	建筑物 141	jiàn zhù wù 141	jiann juh wuh 141
142 bullet	子弹 142	zǐ dàn 142	tzyy dann 142
143 burn	烧 143	shāo 143	shau 143
144 business	买卖 144	mǎi mài 144	mae may 144
145 butcher	肉店 145	ròu diàn 145	row diann 145
146 butter	黄油 146	huáng yóu 146	hwang you 146
147 butterfly	蝴蝶 147	hú dié 147	hwu dye 147
148 button	扣子 148	kòuzi 148	kowtz 148
149 buy	买 149	mǎi 149	mae 149
150 cabbage	洋白菜 150	yáng bái cài 150	yang bair tsay 150
151 cake	糕 151	gāo 151	gau 151
152 calf	犊子 152	dúzi 152	dwutz 152
153 call	叫 153	jiào 153	jiaw 153
154 camp	野营 154	yě yíng 154	yee yng 154
155 candle	蜡烛 155	là zhú 155	lah jwu 155
156 capital	首都 156	shǒu dū 156	shoou du 156
157 capsize	倾复 157	qīng fù 157	ching fuh 157
158 capture	捕获 158	bǔ huò 158	buu huoh 158
159 car	车 159	chē 159	che 159
160 cardboard	纸板 160	zhǐ bǎn 160	jyy baan 160

English	Simplified Chinese	Pinyin (with tone-accents)	Romanized transliteration
161 careful	小心 161	xiǎo xīn 161	sheau shin 161
162 cargo	货物 162	huò wù 162	huoh wuh 162
163 carnation	荷兰石竹 163	hé lán shí zhú 163	her lan shyr jwu 163
164 carpet	地毯 164	dì tǎn 164	dih taan 164
165 carrot	胡萝卜 165	hú luóbo 165	hwu luo-bo 165
166 carry	搬 166	bān 166	ban 166
167 cash	现款 167	xiàn kuǎn 167	shiann koan 167
168 cat	猫 168	māo 168	mhau 168
169 catch	抓住 169	zhuā zhù 169	jua juh 169
170 cattle	家畜 170	jiā chù 170	jia chuh 170
171 cauliflower	菜花 171	cài huā 171	tsay hua 171
172 caution	谨慎 172	jǐn shèn 172	jiin shenn 172
173 cellar	地下室 173	dì xià shì 173	dih shiah shyh 173
174 cemetery	坟地 174	fén dì 174	fern dih 174
175 century	世纪 175	shì jì 175	shyh jih 175
176 chain	链子 176	liànzi 176	lianntz 176
177 chair	椅子 177	yǐzi 177	yiitz 177
178 chance	机会 178	jī huì 178	ji huey 178
179 change	变化 179	biàn huà 179	biann huah 179
180 cheap	便宜 180	piányi 180	pyan-yi 180

English	Simplified Chinese	Pinyin (with tone-accents)	Romanized transliteration
181 cheek	腮 181	sāi 181	sai 181
182 cheese	干酪 182	gān lào 182	gan law 182
183 cherry	樱桃 183	yīng táo 183	ing taur 183
184 chess	棋 184	qí 184	chyi 184
185 chest	胸膛 185	xiōng táng 185	shiong tarng 185
186 chicken	鸡 186	jī 186	ji 186
187 child	小孩 187	xiǎo hái 187	sheau hair 187
188 chimney	烟筒 188	yāntong 188	ian-toong 188
189 chin	下巴 189	xiàba 189	shiah-ba 189
190 Christmas	圣诞节 190	shèng dàn jié 190	sheng dann jye 190
191 church	教堂 191	jiào táng 191	jiaw tarng 191
192 cider	苹果酒 192	píng guǒ jiǔ 192	pyng guoo jeou 192
193 circle	圆 193	yuán 193	yuan 193
194 citizen	市民 194	shì mín 194	shyh min 194
195 clean	干净 195	gān jìng 195	gan jinq 195
196 clear	清楚 196	qīng chǔ 196	ching chuu 196
197 clergy	牧师 197	mù shī 197	muh shy 197
198 climb	登 198	dēng 198	deng 198
199 close	关 199	guān 199	guan 199
200 clothing	衣服 200	yī fú 200	i fwu 200

English	Simplified Chinese	Pinyin (with tone-accents)	Romanized transliteration
201 cloud	云彩 201	yún cǎi 201	yun tsae 201
202 coal	煤 202	méi 202	mei 202
203 coat	外衣 203	wài yī 203	way i 203
204 cockroach	蟑螂 204	zhāngláng 204	jang-lang 204
205 codfish	鳕鱼 205	xuě yú 205	sheue yu 205
206 cold	寒冷 206	hán lěng 206	harn leeng 206
207 collar	衣领 207	yī lǐng 207	i liing 207
208 color	颜色 208	yán sè 208	yan seh 208
209 comb	梳子 209	shūzi 209	shutz 209
210 come	来 210	lái 210	lai 210
211 comfort	安慰 211	ān wèi 211	an wey 211
212 compartment	分隔间 212	fēn gé jiān 212	fen ger jian 212
213 competition	竞赛 213	jìng sài 213	jinq say 213
214 condition	条件 214	tiáo jiàn 214	tyau jiann 214
215 connection	关系 215	guānxi 215	guan-shih 215
216 constipation	便秘 216	biàn bì 216	biann bih 216
217 contagious	传染性 217	chuán rǎn xìng 217	chwan raan shinq 217
218 cook	炊事员 218	chuī shì yuán 218	chuei shyh yuan 218
219 copper	铜 219	tóng 219	torng 219
220 cord	软线 220	ruǎn xiàn 220	roan shiann 220

English	Simplified Chinese	Pinyin (with tone-accents)	Romanized transliteration
221 corkscrew	开塞钻 221	kāi sāi zuàn 221	kai sai tzuann 221
222 corn (maize)	玉米 222	yù mǐ 222	yuh mii 222
223 correct	正确 223	zhèng què 223	jenq chiueh 223
224 cost	费用 224	fèiyong 224	fey-yonq 224
225 cotton	棉布 225	mián bù 225	mian buh 225
226 couch	长沙发椅 226	cháng shā fā yǐ 226	charng sha fa yii 226
227 cough	咳嗽 227	ké sòu 227	ker sow 227
228 count	算 228	suàn 228	suann 228
229 country	国家 229	guó jiā 229	gwo jia 229
230 courage	勇气 230	yǒng qì 230	yeong chih 230
231 cousin	堂兄弟 231	táng xiōng di 231	tarng shiong dih 231
232 cow	母牛 232	mǔ niú 232	muu niou 232
233 cracker	咸饼 233	xián bǐng 233	shyan biing 233
234 crane	起重机 234	qǐ zhòng jī 234	chii jonq ji 234
235 crawl	爬 235	pá 235	par 235
236 crazy	疯狂 236	fēng kuáng 236	feng kwang 236
237 cream	奶脂 237	nǎi zhī 237	nae jy 237
238 crib	小床 238	xiǎo chuáng 238	sheau chwang 238
239 crime	犯罪 239	fàn zuì 239	fann tzuey 239
240 cripple	跛子 240	bǒzi 240	bootz 240

English	Simplified Chinese	Pinyin (with tone-accents)	Romanized transliteration
241 cry	哭 241	kū 241	ku 241
242 cucumber	黄瓜 242	huáng guā 242	hwang gua 242
243 cup	杯子 243	bēizi 243	beitz 243
244 curtain	窗帘 244	chuāng lián 244	chuang lian 244
245 customs	海关 245	hǎi guān 245	hae guan 245
246 cut	切 246	qiē 246	chie 246
247 damage	损害 247	sǔn hài 247	soen hay 247
248 danger	危险 248	wēi xiǎn 248	uei shean 248
249 dark	黑暗 249	hēi àn 249	hei ann 249
250 daughter	女儿 250	nǚ ér 250	neu erl 250
251 day	天 251	tiān 251	tian 251
252 deaf	聋子 252	lóngzi 252	longtz 252
253 death	死 253	sǐ 253	syy 253
254 debt	借款 254	jiè kuǎn 254	jieh koan 254
255 December	十二月 255	shí èr yuè 255	shyr ell yueh 255
256 deep	深 256	shēn 256	shen 256
257 defective	有毛病 257	yǒu máo bìng 257	yeou mau binq 257
258 degree	程度 258	chéng dù 258	cherng duh 258
259 deliver	送 259	sòng 259	song 259
260 dentist	牙医 260	yá yī 260	ya i 260

English	Simplified Chinese	Pinyin (with tone-accents)	Romanized transliteration
261 departure	出发 261	chū fā 261	chu fa 261
262 desert	沙漠 262	shā mò 262	sha moh 262
263 dessert	点心 263	diǎn xīn 263	dean shin 263
264 destroy	破坏 264	pò huài 264	poh huay 264
265 detour	弯路 265	wān lù 265	uan luh 265
266 diaper (baby's napkin)	尿布 266	niào bù 266	niaw buh 266
267 diarrhea	闹肚子 267	nào dùzi 267	naw duhtz 267
268 dictionary	辞典 268	cí diǎn 268	tsyr dean 268
269 different	不同 269	bù tóng 269	buh torng 269
270 digestion	消化 270	xiāo huà 270	shiau huah 270
271 dining room	食堂 271	shí táng 271	shyr tarng 271
272 dinner	晚餐 272	wǎn cān 272	woan tsan 272
273 direction	方向 273	fāng xiàng 273	fang shiang 273
274 dirty	脏 274	zāng 274	tzang 274
275 disappear	消失 275	xiāo shī 275	shiau shy 275
276 dish	盘子 276	pánzi 276	parntz 276
277 distance	距离 277	jù lí 277	jiuh li 277
278 dive	跳人 278	tiào rù 278	tiaw ruh 278
279 divide	划分 279	huà fēn 279	huah fen 279
280 divorce	离婚 280	lí hūn 280	li huen 280

English		Simplified Chinese	Pinyin (with tone-accents)	Romanized transliteration
281	document	文件 281	wén jiàn 281	wen jiann 281
282	dog	狗 282	gǒu 282	goou 282
283	doll	玩偶 283	wán ǒu 283	wan oou 283
284	donkey	驴 284	lǘ 284	liu 284
285	door	门 285	mén 285	men 285
286	doubt	怀疑 286	huái yí 286	hwai yi 286
287	down	向下 287	xiàng xià 287	shiang shiah 287
288	dowry	陪嫁钱 288	péi jià qián 288	peir jiah chyan 288
289	drawing	素描 289	sù miáo 289	suh miau 289
290	dream	梦 290	mèng 290	menq 290
291	dress	连衣裙 291	lián yī qún 291	lian i chiun 291
292	drink	喝 292	hē 292	he 292
293	drive	开 293	kāi 293	kai 293
294	driver	司机 294	sī jī 294	sy ji 294
295	drop	掉 295	diào 295	diaw 295
296	drown	淹 296	yān 296	ian 296
297	drug	药品 297	yào pǐn 297	yaw piin 297
298	drum	鼓 298	gǔ 298	guu 298
299	dry	干燥 299	gān zào 299	gan tzaw 299
300	duck	鸭子 300	yāzi 300	iatz 300

English	Simplified Chinese	Pinyin (with tone-accents)	Romanized transliteration
301 dust	灰尘 301	huī chén 301	huei chern 301
302 duty	义务 302	yì wù 302	yih wuh 302
303 ear	耳朵 303	ěrduo 303	eel-duoo 303
304 early	早 304	zǎo 304	tzao 304
305 earring	耳环 305	ěr huán 305	eel hwan 305
306 earth	地球 306	dì qiú 306	dih chyou 306
307 earthquake	地震 307	dì zhèn 307	dih jenn 307
308 east	东边 308	dōng biān 308	dong bian 308
309 easy	容易 309	róng yì 309	rong yih 309
310 eat	吃 310	chī 310	chy 310
311 effort	努力 311	nǔ lì 311	nuu lih 311
312 egg	鸡蛋 312	jī dàn 312	ji dann 312
313 eight	八 313	bā 313	ba 313
314 eighteen	十八 314	shí bā 314	shyr ba 314
315 eighty	八十 315	bā shí 315	ba shyr 315
316 elbow	肘 316	zhǒu 316	joou 316 ˇ
317 elevator (lift)	电梯 317	diàn tī 317	diann ti 317
318 eleven	十一 318	shí yī 318	shyr i 318
319 empty	空 319	kōng 319	kong 319
320 enemy	敌人 320	dí rén 320	dyi ren 320

English	Simplified Chinese	Pinyin (with tone-accents)	Romanized transliteration
321 entrance	入口 321	rù kǒu 321	ruh koou 321
322 envelope	信封 322	xìn fēng 322	shinn feng 322
323 evening	傍晚 323	bàng wǎn 323	banq woan 323
324 exchange	交易所 324	jiāo yì suǒ 324	jiau yih suoo 324
325 excuse	辩解 325	biàn jiě 325	biann jiee 325
326 exhibition (display)	展览会 326	zhǎn lǎn huì 326	jaan laan huey 326
327 exit	出口 327	chū kǒu 327	chu koou 327
328 expect	期待 328	qī dài 328	chi day 328
329 expense	费用 329	fèi yòng 329	fey-yonq 329
330 expensive	贵 330	guì 330	guey 330
331 expire	满期 331	mǎn qī 331	maan chi 331
332 extreme	极端 332	jí duān 332	jyi duan 332
333 eye	眼睛 333	yǎn jīng 333	yean jing 333
334 eyeglasses	眼镜 334	yǎn jìng 334	yean jinq 334
335 face	脸 335	liǎn 335	lean 335
336 factory	工厂 336	gōng chǎng 336	gong chaang 336
337 family	家族 337	jiā zú 337	jia tzwu 337
338 far	远 338	yuǎn 338	yeuan 338
339 fare	车费 339	chē fèi 339	che fey 339
340 fast	快 340	kuài 340	kuay 340

English	Simplified Chinese	Pinyin (with tone-accents)	Romanized transliteration
341 fat	脂肪 341	zhī fáng 341	jy farng 341
342 father	父亲 342	fù qīn 342	fuh chin 342
343 fear	害怕 343	hài pà 343	hay pah 343
344 February	二月 344	èr yuè 344	ell yueh 344
345 female	女性 345	nǚ xìng 345	neu shing 345
346 ferry	渡船 346	dù chuán 346	duh chwan 346
347 few	一点 347	yì diǎn 347	yih dean 347
348 fifteen	十五 348	shí wǔ 348	shyr wuu 348
349 fifty	五十 349	wǔ shí 349	wuu shyr 349
350 fig	无花果 350	wú huā guǒ 350	wu hua guoo 350
351 find	发现 351	fā xiàn 351	fa shiann 351
352 finger	手指 352	shǒu zhǐ 352	shoou jyy 352
353 fingernail	指甲 353	zhǐ jiǎ 353	jyy jea 353
354 fire	火 354	huǒ 354	huoo 354
355 fish	鱼 355	yú 355	yu 355
356 fist	拳头 356	quántou 356	chyuan-tou 356
357 five	五 357	wǔ 357	wuu 357
358 flat	平 358	píng 358	pyng 358
359 flea	跳蚤 359	tiào zǎo 359	tiaw tzao 359
360 floor	地板 360	dì bǎn 360	dih baan 360

English	Simplified Chinese	Pinyin (with tone-accents)	Romanized transliteration
361 flour	面粉 361	miàn fěn 361	miann feen 361
362 flower	花 362	huā 362	hua 362
363 fly	苍蝇 363	cāng yíng 363	tsang yng 363
364 fog	雾 364	wù 364	wuh 364
365 food	食物 365	shí wù 365	shyr wuh 365
366 foot	脚 366	jiǎo 366	jeau 366
367 forbidden	被禁止 367	bèi jìn zhǐ 367	bey jin jyy 367
368 foreign	外国 368	wài guó 368	way gwo 368
369 forest	森林 369	sēn lín 369	sen lin 369
370 forget	忘记 370	wàng jì 370	wang jih 370
371 fork	叉子 371	chāzi 371	chatz 371
372 forty	四十 372	sì shí 372	syh shyr 372
373 fountain	泉 373	quán 373	chyuan 373
374 four	四 374	sì 374	syh 374
375 fourteen	十四 375	shí sì 375	shyr syh 375
376 fox	狐狸 376	húli 376	hwu-li 376
377 fragile	脆 377	cuì 377	tsuey 377
378 frame	画框 378	huà kuàng 378	huah kuang 378
379 free	自由 379	zì yóu 379	tzyh you 379
380 fresh	新鲜 380	xīn xiān 380	shin shian 380

English	Simplified Chinese	Pinyin (with tone-accents)	Romanized transliteration
381 Friday	星期五 381	xīng qī wǔ 381	shing chi wuu 381
382 fried fish	油炸鱼 382	yóu zhá yú 382	you jar yu 382
383 friend	朋友 383	péng yǒu 383	perng yeou 383
384 frog	蛙子 384	wāzi 384	uatz 384
385 from	从 385	cóng 385	tsorng 385
386 front	正面 386	zhèng miàn 386	jenq miann 386
387 fruit	水果 387	shuǐ guǒ 387	shoei guoo 387
388 full	充满 388	chōng mǎn 388	chong maan 388
389 funeral	葬礼 389	zàng lǐ 389	tzanq lii 389
390 fur coat	皮外衣 390	pí wài yī 390	pyi way i 390
391 furniture	家具 391	jiā jù 391	jia jiuh 391
392 gain	获得 392	huò dé 392	huoh der 392
393 gall-bladder	胆囊 393	dǎn náng 393	daan nang 393
394 game	比赛 394	bǐ sài 394	bii say 394
395 garbage	垃圾 395	lā jī 395	lha ji 395
396 garden	院子 396	yuànzi 396	yuanntz 396
397 garlic	大蒜 397	dà suàn 397	dah suann 397
398 garter	吊抹带 398	diào wà dài 398	diaw wah day 398
399 gasoline (petrol)	汽油 399	qì yóu 399	chih you 399
400 general delivery	存局候领的邮件 400	cún jú hòu lǐngdi yóu jiàn 400	tswen jyu how liing-dih you jiann 400

English	Simplified Chinese	Pinyin (with tone-accents)	Romanized transliteration
401 genuine	真 401	zhēn 401	jen 401
402 gift	礼物 402	lǐ wù 402	lii wuh 402
403 girl	女孩子 403	nǚ háizi 403	neu hairtz 403
404 give	给 404	gěi 404	geei 404
405 glad	高兴 405	gāo xìng 405	gau shinq 405
406 glass	玻璃 406	bōli 406	bo-li 406
407 glove	手套 407	shǒu tào 407	shoou taw 407
408 glue	胶 408	jiāo 408	jiau 408
409 go	去 409	qù 409	chiuh 409
410 goat	山羊 410	shān yáng 410	shan yang 410
411 God	上帝 411	shàng dì 411	shanq dih 411
412 gold	金 412	jīn 412	jin 412
413 good	好 413	hǎo 413	hao 413
414 goodbye	再见 414	zài jiàn 414	tzay jiann 414
415 goose	鹅 415	é 415	er 415
416 grape	葡萄 416	pútao 416	pwu-taur 416
417 grapefruit	柚子 417	yòuzi 417	yowtz 417
418 grass	草 418	cǎo 418	tsao 418
419 gravy	肉汁 419	ròu zhī 419	row jy 419
420 green	绿色 420	lù sè 420	liuh seh 420

English		Simplified Chinese	Pinyin (with tone-accents)	Romanized transliteration
421	grey	灰色 421	huī sè 421	huei seh 421
422	growing	成长 422	chéng zhǎng 422	cherng jaang 422
423	guaranty	保证 423	bǎo zhèng 423	bao jenq 423
424	guest	客人 424	kè rén 424	keh ren 424
425	guide	带路人 425	dài lù rén 425	day luh ren 425
426	guilty	有罪 426	yǒu zuì 426	yeou tzuey 426
427	habit	习惯 427	xí guàn 427	shyi guann 427
428	hail	霰 428	xiàn 428	shiann 428
429	hair	头发 429	tóu fā 429	tour fa 429
430	hairdresser	理发师 430	lǐ fā shī 430	lii fa shy 430
431	half	一半 431	yí bàn 431	yi bann 431
432	ham	火腿 432	huǒ tuǐ 432	huoo toei 432
433	hammer	锤子 433	chuízi 433	chweitz 433
434	hand	手 434	shǒu 434	shoou 434
435	handkerchief	手巾 435	shǒu jīn 435	shoou jin 435
436	hang	挂 436	guà 436	guah 436
437	harbor	港口 437	gǎng kǒu 437	gaang koou 437
438	hard	硬 438	yìng 438	yinq 438
439	harvest	收获 439	shōu huò 439	shou huoh 439
440	hat	帽子 440	màozi 440	mawtz 440

English	Simplified Chinese	Pinyin (with tone-accents)	Romanized transliteration
441 hate	憎恨 441	zēng hèn 441	tzeng henn 441
442 have	有 442	yǒu 442	yeou 442
443 he	他 443	tā 443	ta 443
444 head	头 444	tóu 444	tour 444
445 health	健康 445	jiàn kāng 445	jiann kang 445
446 hear	听 446	tīng 446	ting 446
447 heart	心脏 447	xīn zàng 447	shin tzang 447
448 heavy	重 448	zhòng 448	jonq 448
449 heel	脚后跟 449	jiǎo hòu gēn 449	jeau how gen 449
450 help	帮助 450	bāng zhù 450	bang juh 450
451 here	这里 451	zhè lǐ 451	jeh lii 451
452 herring	鲱鱼 452	fēi yú 452	fei yu 452
453 highway	公路 453	gōng lù 453	gong luh 453
454 hole	孔 454	kǒng 454	koong 454
455 holiday	节日 455	jié rì 455	jye ryh 455
456 honey	蜂蜜 456	fēng mì 456	feng mih 456
457 horse	马 457	mǎ 457	maa 457
458 horserace	赛马 458	sài mǎ 458	say maa 458
459 hospital	医院 459	yī yuàn 459	i yuann 459
460 hot	热 460	rè 460	reh 460

English	Simplified Chinese	Pinyin (with tone-accents)	Romanized transliteration
461 hour	小时 461	xiǎo shí 461	sheau shyr 461
462 house	房子 462	fángzi 462	farngtz 462
463 how are you?	你好吗? 463	nǐ hǎoma? 463	nii hao-ma? 463
464 how much?	多少钱? 464	duō shǎo qián? 464	duo shao chyan? 464
465 hundred	百 465	bǎi 465	bae 465
466 hungry	饿 466	è 466	eh 466
467 hunt	打猎 467	dǎ liè 467	daa lieh 467
468 husband	丈夫 468	zhàngfu 468	janq-fu 468
469 ice	冰 469	bīng 469	bing 469
470 ice cream	冰淇淋 470	bīng qí lín 470	bing chyi lin 470
471 illegal	违法 471	wéi fǎ 471	wei faa 471
472 illness	病 472	bìng 472	binq 472
473 information	消息 473	xiāo xī 473	shiau shi 473
474 ink	墨水 474	mò shuǐ 474	moh shoei 474
475 insect	昆虫 475	kūn chóng 475	kuen chorng 475
476 insurance	保险 476	bǎo xiǎn 476	bao shean 476
477 interest	利息 477	lì xī 477	lih shi 477
478 interpreter	翻译 478	fān yì 478	fan yih 478
479 invention	发明 479	fā míng 479	fa ming 479
480 iron	铁 480	tiě 480	tiee 480

	English	Simplified Chinese	Pinyin (with tone-accents)	Romanized transliteration
481	ironing	熨 481	yùn 481	yunn 481
482	island	海岛 482	hǎi dǎo 482	hae dao 482
483	jam (marmalade)	果酱 483	guǒ jiàng 483	guoo jianq 483
484	January	一月 484	yí yuè 484	yi yueh 484
485	jealous	嫉妒 485	jídu 485	jyi-duh 485
486	jewel	宝石 486	bǎo shí 486	bao shyr 486
487	joke	笑话 487	xiàohua 487	shiaw-huah 487
488	July	七月 488	qī yuè 488	chi yueh 488
489	June	六月 489	liù yuè 489	liow yueh 489
490	key	钥匙 490	yàoshi 490	yaw-shy 490
491	kidney	肾脏 491	shèn zàng 491	shenn tzanq 491
492	kiss	接吻 492	jiē wěn 492	jie woen 492
493	kitchen	厨房 493	chú fáng 493	chwu farng 493
494	knapsack	背包 494	bēi bāo 494	bei bau 494
495	knee	膝 495	xī 495	shi 495
496	knife	小刀子 496	xiǎo dāozi 496	sheau dautz 496
497	lace	花边 497	huā biān 497	hua bian 497
498	ladder	梯子 498	tīzi 498	titz 498
499	lake	湖 499	hú 499	hwu 499
500	lamb	羊羔 500	yáng gāo 500	yang gau 500

English	Simplified Chinese	Pinyin (with tone-accents)	Romanized transliteration
501 language	语言 501	yǔ yán 501	yeu yan 501
502 large	大 502	dà 502	dah 502
503 late	晚 503	wǎn 503	woan 503
504 laugh	笑 504	xiào 504	shiaw 504
505 laundry	洗衣店 505	xǐ yī diàn 505	shii i diann 505
506 lawn	草坪 506	cǎo píng 506	tsao pyng 506
507 lawyer	律师 507	lǜ shī 507	liuh shy 507
508 lazy	懒惰 508	lǎn duò 508	laan duoh 508
509 lead	铅 509	qiān 509	chian 509
510 leaf	叶子 510	yèzi 510	yehtz 510
511 learn	学习 511	xué xí 511	shyue shyi 511
512 leather	皮革 512	pí gé 512	pyi ger 512
513 leave (to depart)	离开 513	lí kāi 513	li kai 513
514 left	左边 514	zuǒbian 514	tzuoo-bian 514
515 leg	腿 515	tuǐ 515	toei 515
516 lens	透镜 516	tòu jìng 516	tow jinq 516
517 letter	信 517	xìn 517	shinn 517
518 lie	谎话 518	huǎng huà 518	hoang huah 518
519 life	生命 519	shēng mìng 519	sheng minq 519
520 life belt	安全带 520	ān quán dài 520	an chyuan day 520

English	Simplified Chinese	Pinyin (with tone-accents)	Romanized transliteration
521 light	光 521	guāng 521	guang 521
522 light bulb	电灯泡 522	diàn dēng pào 522	diann deng paw 522
523 lightning	闪电 523	shǎn diàn 523	shaan diann 523
524 lilac	丁香花 524	dīng xiāng huā 524	ding shiang hua 524
525 linen	亚麻布 525	yà má bù 525	yah ma buh 525
526 lion	狮子 526	shīzi 526	shytz 526
527 lip	嘴唇 527	zuǐ chún 527	tzoei chwen 527
528 liquid	液体 528	yè tǐ 528	yeh tii 528
529 liver	肝脏 529	gān zàng 529	gan tzanq 529
530 lobster	龙虾 530	lóng xiā 530	long shia 530
531 lock	锁 531	suǒ 531	suoo 531
532 long	长 532	cháng 532	charng 532
533 loss	损失 533	sǔn shī 533	soen shy 533
534 louse	虱子 534	shīzi 534	shytz 534
535 love	爱 535	ài 535	ay 535
536 lubricating	上油 536	shàng yóu 536	shanq you 536
537 luck	运气 537	yùnqi 537	yunn-chih 537
538 lunch	午饭 538	wǔ fàn 538	wuu fann 538
539 lung	肺脏 539	fèi zàng 539	fey tzanq 539
540 magazine	杂志 540	zá zhì 540	tzar jyh 540

English	Simplified Chinese	Pinyin (with tone-accents)	Romanized transliteration
541 magic	魔术 541	mó shù 541	mo shuh 541
542 maid	女仆 542	nǚ pú 542	neu pwu 542
543 mail	邮件 543	yóu jiàn 543	you jiann 543
544 make	做 544	zuò 544	tzuoh 544
545 male	男性 545	nán xìng 545	nan shinq 545
546 malicious	恶意 546	è yì 546	eh yih 546
547 man	男人 547	nán rén 547	nan ren 547
548 map	地图 548	dì tú 548	dih twu 548
549 marble	大理石 549	dà lǐ shí 549	dah lii shyr 549
550 March	三月 550	sān yuè 550	san yueh 550
551 market	市场 551	shì chǎng 551	shyh chaang 551
552 marriage	结婚 552	jié hūn 552	jye huen 552
553 match	火柴 553	huǒ chái 553	huoo chair 553
554 mattress	床垫 554	rù diàn 554	ruh diann 554
555 May	五月 555	wǔ yuè 555	wuu yueh 555
556 maybe	也许 556	yě xǔ 556	yee sheu 556
557 mayor	市长 557	shì zhǎng 557	shyh jaang 557
558 meal	饭 558	fàn 558	fann 558
559 meat	肉 559	ròu 559	row 559
560 medicine	药 560	yào 560	yaw 560

English		Simplified Chinese	Pinyin (with tone-accents)	Romanized transliteration
561	meet	遇见 561	yù jiàn 561	yuh jiann 561
562	member	会员 562	huì yuán 562	huey yuan 562
563	menu	菜单 563	cài dān 563	tsay dan 563
564	merchant	商人 564	shāng rén 564	shang ren 564
565	merry	欢乐 565	huān lè 565	huan leh 565
566	middle	中间 566	zhōng jiān 566	jong jian 566
567	milk	牛奶 567	niú nǎi 567	niou nae 567
568	mirror	镜子 568	jìngzi 568	jinqtz 568
569	Miss	小姐 569	xiǎo jiě 569	sheau jiee 569
570	mistake	错误 570	cuò wù 570	tsuoh wuh 570
571	Monday	星期一 571	xīng qī yī 571	shing chi i 571
572	money	货币 572	huò bì 572	huoh bih 572
573	month	月 573	yuè 573	yueh 573
574	moon	月亮 574	yuèliang 574	yueh-liang 574
575	more	更多 575	gèng duō 575	genq duo 575
576	morning	早晨 576	zǎo chén 576	tzao chern 576
577	mosquito	蚊子 577	wénzi 577	wentz 577
578	mother	母亲 578	mǔqin 578	muu-chin 578
579	mountain	山 579	shān 579	shan 579
580	mouse	鼹鼠 580	xī shǔ 580	shi shuu 580

English	Simplified Chinese	Pinyin (with tone-accents)	Romanized transliteration
581 mouth	嘴 581	zuǐ 581	tzoei 581
582 move	动 582	dòng 582	donq 582
583 movie	电影 583	diàn yǐng 583	diann yiing 583
584 Mr (addressing)	先生 584	xiānsheng 584	shiang-sheng 584
585 Mrs (addressing)	夫人 585	fū rén 585	fu ren 585
586 much	许多 586	xǔ duō 586	sheu duo 586
587 muscle	肌肉 587	jī ròu 587	ji row 587
588 mushroom	蘑菇 588	mógu 588	mo-gu 588
589 mustard	芥黄 589	jiè huáng 589	jieh hwang 589
590 mute	哑巴 590	yǎba 590	yea-ba 590
591 mutual	互相 591	hù xiàng 591	huh shiang 591
592 nail	钉子 592	dīngzi 592	dingtz 592
593 naked	赤裸裸 593	chì luǒ luǒ 593	chyh luoo luoo 593
594 name	名字 594	míngzi 594	mingtz 594
595 narrow	窄 595	zhǎi 595	jae 595
596 near	近 596	jìn 596	jinn 596
597 neck	脖子 597	bózi 597	bortz 597
598 necklace	项链 598	xiàng liàn 598	shiang liann 598
599 need	必要 599	bì yào 599	bih yaw 599
600 needle	针 600	zhēn 600	jen 600

English	Simplified Chinese	Pinyin (with tone-accents)	Romanized transliteration
601 negligent	疏忽 601	shūhu 601	shu-hu 601
602 neighbor	邻居 602	lín jū 602	lin jiu 602
603 net (fishing)	网 603	wǎng 603	woang 603
604 never	决不 604	jué bù 604	jyue buh 604
605 new	新 605	xīn 605	shin 605
606 newspaper	报纸 606	bào zhǐ 606	baw jyy 606
607 night	晚上 607	wǎnshang 607	woan-shang 607
608 nine	九 608	jiǔ 608	jeou 608
609 nineteen	十九 609	shí jiǔ 609	shyr jeou 609
610 ninety	九十 610	jiǔ shí 610	jeou shyr 610
611 no	不 611	bù 611	buh 611
612 noise	噪音 612	zào yīn 612	tzaw in 612
613 noodle	面条 613	miàn tiáo 613	miann tyau 613
614 noon	中午 614	zhōng wǔ 614	jong wuu 614
615 north	北边 615	běi biān 615	beei bian 615
616 nose	鼻子 616	bízi 616	byitz 616
617 November	十一月 617	shí yī yuè 617	shyr i yueh 617
618 now	现在 618	xiàn zài 618	shiann tzay 618
619 number	数字 619	shù zì 619	shuh tzyh 619
620 nurse	护士 620	hùshi 620	huhrshyh 620

English	Simplified Chinese	Pinyīn (with tone-accents)	Romanized transliteration
621 nut	坚果 621	jiān guǒ 621	jian guoo 621
622 oak	栎树 622	lì shù 622	lih shuh 622
623 oar	橹 623	lǔ 623	luu 623
624 oats	燕麦 624	yàn mài 624	yann may 624
625 occupy	占 625	zhàn 625	jann 625
626 October	十月 626	shí yuè 626	shyr yueh 626
627 office	办事处 627	bàn shì chù 627	bann shyh chuh 627
628 oil	油 628	yóu 628	you 628
629 old	旧 629	jiù 629	jiow 629
630 one	一 630	yī 630	i 630
631 onion	洋葱 631	yáng cōng 631	yang tsong 631
632 only	只 632	zhǐ 632	jyy 632
633 open	开的 633	kāide 633	kai-de 633
634 or	或者 634	huò zhě 634	huoh jee 634
635 orange	桔子 635	júzi 635	jyutz 635
636 other	其他 636	qí tā 636	chyi ta 636
637 outside	外 637	wài 637	way 637
638 ox	公牛 638	gōng niú 638	gong niou 638
639 page	页 639	yè 639	yeh 639
640 pain	痛苦 640	tòng kǔ 640	tonq kuu 640

English	Simplified Chinese	Pinyin (with tone-accents)	Romanized transliteration
641 painting	绘画 641	huì huà 641	huey huah 641
642 pair	对 642	duì 642	duey 642
643 pale	苍白 643	cāng bái 643	tsang bair 643
644 pancake	煎饼 644	jiānbǐng 644	jian-biing 644
645 paper	纸 645	zhǐ 645	jyy 645
646 parachute	降落伞 646	jiàng luò sǎn 646	jianq luoh saan 646
647 parcel	包裹 647	bāo guǒ 647	bau guoo 647
648 parents	父母 648	fù mǔ 648	fuh muu 648
649 parking	停车 649	tíng chē 649	tyng che 649
650 parsley	欧芹 650	ōu qín 650	ou chyn 650
651 part	部分 651	bùfen 651	buh-fen 651
652 pastry	糕点 652	gāo diǎn 652	gau dean 652
653 patience	忍耐 653	rěn nài 653	reen nay 653
654 pay	交钱 654	jiāo qián 654	jiau chyan 654
655 pea	豌豆 655	wān dòu 655	uan dow 655
656 peace	和平 656	hé píng 656	her pyng 656
657 pear	梨子 657	lízi 657	litz 657
658 peasant	农民 658	nóng mín 658	nong min 658
659 pen	钢笔 659	gāng bǐ 659	gang bii 659
660 pencil	铅笔 660	qiān bǐ 660	chian bii 660

English	Simplified Chinese	Pinyin (with tone-accents)	Romanized transliteration
661 pepper	胡椒 661	hú jiāo 661	hwu jiau 661
662 permission	许可 662	xǔ kě 662	sheu kee 662
663 perspire	出汗 663	chū hàn 663	chu hann 663
664 persuade	说服 664	shuō fú 664	shuo fwu 664
665 pharmacy	药房 665	yào fáng 665	yaw farng 665
666 physician	医生 666	yī shēng 666	i sheng 666
667 picture	画 667	huà 667	huah 667
668 piece	一个 668	yíge 668	yi-geh 668
669 pig	猪 669	zhū 669	ju 669
670 pigeon	鸽子 670	gēzi 670	getz 670
671 pillow	枕头 671	zhěntou 671	jeen-tou 671
672 pin	别针 672	bié zhēn 672	bye jen 672
673 pine tree	松树 673	sōng shù 673	song shuh 673
674 pink	粉红色 674	fěn hóng sè 674	feen horng seh 674
675 pipe (tube)	导管 675	dǎo guǎn 675	dao goan 675
676 plant	植物 676	zhí wù 676	jyr wuh 676
677 platform	站台 677	zhàn tái 677	jann tair 677
678 play	玩 678	wán 678	wan 678
679 playing card	扑克 679	pū kè 679	pu keh 679
680 pleasant	愉快 680	yú kuài 680	yu kuay 680

	English	Simplified Chinese	Pinyin (with tone-accents)	Romanized transliteration
681	please	请 681	qǐng 681	chiing 681
682	pleasure	快乐 682	kuài lè 682	kuay leh 682
683	plier(s)	钳子 683	qiánzi 683	chyantz 683
684	plum	李子 684	lǐzi 684	liitz 684
685	pocket	口袋 685	kǒudai 685	koou-day 685
686	point	点 686	diǎn 686	dean 686
687	poison	毒 687	dú 687	dwu 687
688	poor	穷 688	qióng 688	chyong 688
689	pork	猪肉 689	zhū ròu 689	ju row 689
690	portable	手提式 690	shǒu tí shì 690	shoou tyi shyh 690
691	porter	搬运人 691	bān yùn rén 691	ban yunn ren 691
692	postcard	明信片 692	míng xìn piàn 692	ming shinn piann 692
693	post office	邮局 693	yóu jú 693	you jyu 693
694	pot	锅 694	guō 694	guo 694
695	potato	土豆 695	tǔ dòu 695	tuu dow 695
696	powder	粉末 696	fěn mò 696	feen moh 696
697	price	价钱 697	jiàqian 697	jiah-chyan 697
698	printing	印刷 698	yìn shuā 698	yinn shua 698
699	prison	监狱 699	jiān yù 699	jian yuh 699
700	profession	职业 700	zhí yè 700	jyr yeh 700

English	Simplified Chinese	Pinyin (with tone-accents)	Romanized transliteration
701 property	财产 701	cái chǎn 701	tsair chaan 701
702 purse	钱包 702	qián bāo 702	chyan bau 702
703 quarter	四分之一 703	sì fēn zhī yī 703	syh fen jy i 703
704 question	问题 704	wèn tí 704	wenn tyi 704
705 quick	迅速 705	xùn sù 705	shiunn suh 705
706 quiet	安静 706	ān jìng 706	an jing 706
707 rabbit	兔子 707	tùzi 707	tuhtz 707
708 rag	破布 708	pò bù 708	poh buh 708
709 rain	雨 709	yǔ 709	yeu 709
710 raincoat	雨衣 710	yǔ yī 710	yeu i 710
711 rat	老鼠 711	lǎo shǔ 711	lao shuu 711
712 raw	生 712	shēng 712	sheng 712
713 razor	刮脸刀 713	guā liǎn dāo 713	gua lean dau 713
714 read	读 714	dú 714	dwu 714
715 receipt	收据 715	shōu jù 715	shou jiuh 715
716 red	红 716	hóng 716	horng 716
717 reduce	减少 717	jiǎn shǎo 717	jean shao 717
718 registered	挂号 718	guà hào 718	guah haw 718
719 relax	放松 719	fàng sōng 719	fanq song 719
720 remain	留 720	liú 720	liou 720

English	Simplified Chinese	Pinyin (with tone-accents)	Romanized transliteration
721 remember	想起 721	xiǎngqi 721	sheang-chii 721
722 rent	房租 722	fáng zū 722	farng tzu 722
723 repeat	重复 723	chóng fù 723	chorng fuh 723
724 rescue	救援 724	jiù yuán 724	jiow yuan 724
725 return	回 725	huí 725	hwei 725
726 rich	富裕 726	fù yù 726	fuh yuh 726
727 rifle	步枪 727	bù qiāng 727	buh chiang 727
728 right	右边 728	yòubian 728	yow-bian 728
729 ring	戒指 729	jièzhi 729	jieh-jyy 729
730 ripe	成熟 730	chéng shú 730	cherng shwu 730
731 rise	起立 731	qǐ lì 731	chii lih 731
732 risk	危险 732	wēi xiǎn 732	uei shean 732
733 river	河 733	hé 733	her 733
734 roast	烤 734	kǎo 734	kao 734
735 roof	屋顶 735	wū dǐng 735	u diing 735
736 room	屋子 736	wūzi 736	utz 736
737 root	根 737	gēn 737	gen 737
738 rope	绳子 738	shéngzi 738	sherngtz 738
739 round	圆 739	yuán 739	yuan 739
740 rubber	橡胶 740	xiàng jiāo 740	shiang jiau 740

English	Simplified Chinese	Pinyin (with tone-accents)	Romanized transliteration
741 run	跑 741	pǎo 741	pao 741
742 runway	跑道 742	pǎo dào 742	pao daw 742
743 rusty	生锈的 743	shēng xiùde 743	sheng shiow-de 743
744 sad	悲哀 744	bēi āi 744	bei ai 744
745 saddle	鞍 745	ān 745	an 745
746 safety	安全 746	ān quán 746	an chyuan 746
747 sailor	水手 747	shuǐ shǒu 747	shoei shoou 747
748 salt	盐 748	yán 748	yan 748
749 sample	样品 749	yàng pǐn 749	yanq piin 749
750 sand	沙子 750	shāzi 750	shatz 750
751 Saturday	星期六 751	xīng qī liù 751	shing chi liow 751
752 sausage	香肠 752	xiāng cháng 752	shiang charng 752
753 saw	锯子 753	jùzi 753	jiuhtz 753
754 scarf	围巾 754	wéi jīn 754	wei jin 754
755 school	学校 755	xué xiào 755	shyue shiaw 755
756 science	科学 756	kē xué 756	ke shyue 756
757 scissors	剪子 757	jiǎnzi 757	jeantz 757
758 scrambled eggs	炒鸡蛋 758	chǎo jī dàn 758	chao ji dann 758
759 screw	螺丝 759	luó sī 759	luo sy 759
760 sea	海 760	hǎi 760	hae 760

English	Simplified Chinese	Pinyin (with tone-accents)	Romanized transliteration
761 seasick	晕船 761	yùn chuán 761	yunn chwan 761
762 season	季节 762	jì jié 762	jih jye 762
763 second-hand	半旧 763	bàn jiù 763	bann jiow 763
764 secret	秘密 764	mì mì 764	mih mih 764
765 secure	可靠 765	kě kào 765	kee kaw 765
766 see	看见 766	kàn jiàn 766	kann jiann 766
767 seed	籽 767	zǐ 767	tzyy 767
768 sell	卖 768	mài 768	may 768
769 send	送 769	sòng 769	sonq 769
770 September	九月 770	jiǔ yuè 770	jeou yueh 770
771 serious	认真 771	rèn zhēn 771	renn jen 771
772 seven	七 772	qī 772	chi 772
773 seventeen	十七 773	shí qī 773	shyr chi 773
774 seventy	七十 774	qī shí 774	chi shyr 774
775 sewing	缝纫 775	féng rèn 775	ferng renn 775
776 shark	鲨鱼 776	shā yú 776	sha yu 776
777 shave	刮脸 777	guā liǎn 777	gua lean 777
778 she	她 778	tā 778	ta 778
779 sheep	羊 779	yáng 779	yang 779
780 sheets	床单 780	chuáng dān 780	chwang dan 780

English	Simplified Chinese	Pinyin (with tone-accents)	Romanized transliteration
781 shirt	衬衣 781	chèn yī 781	chenn i 781
782 shoe	鞋 782	xié 782	shye 782
783 short	短 783	duǎn 783	doan 783
784 shoulder	肩膀 784	jiān bǎng 784	jian baang 784
785 show	显示 785	xiǎn shì 785	shean shyh 785
786 shower	淋浴 786	lín yù 786	lin yuh ·786
787 sick	有病 787	yǒu bìng 787	yeou binq 787
788 sidewalk	便道 788	biàn dào 7888	biann daw 788
789 sign	标记 789	biāo jì 789	biau jih 789
790 signature	签名 790	qiān míng 790	chian ming 790
791 silk	丝绸 791	sī chóu 791	sy chour 791
792 silver	银 792	yín 792	yn 792
793 sing	唱 793	chàng 793	chanq 793
794 sister	姐妹 794	jiě mèi 794	jiee mey 794
795 sit	坐 795	zuò 795	tzouh 795
796 six	六 796	liù 796	liow 796
797 sixteen	十六 797	shí liù 797	shyr liow 797
798 sixty	六十 798	liù shí 798	liow shyr 798
799 skin	皮肤 799	pí fū 799	pyi fu 799
800 skirt	裙子 800	qúnzi 800	chyuntz 800

English	Simplified Chinese	Pinyin (with tone-accents)	Romanized transliteration
801 sky	天空 801	tiān kōng 801	tian kong 801
802 sled	雪橇 802	xuě qiāo 802	sheue chiau 802
803 sleep	睡觉 803	shuì jiào 803	shuey jiau 803
804 slowly	慢慢 804	màn màn 804	mann mhan 804
805 small	小 805	xiǎo 805	sheau 805
806 smell	闻 806	wén 806	wen 806
807 smoke	烟 807	yān 807	ian 807
808 snake	蛇 808	shé 808	sher 808
809 snow	雪 809	xuě 809	sheue 809
810 soap	肥皂 810	féi zào 810	feir tzaw 810
811 sober	未喝醉的 811	wèi hē zuìde 811	wey he tzuey-de 811
812 soft	软 812	ruǎn 812	roan 812
813 son	儿子 813	érzi 813	erltz 813
814 song	歌 814	gē 814	ge 814
815 sorrow	悲痛 815	bēi tòng 815	bei tonq 815
816 soup	汤 816	tāng 816	tang 816
817 sour	酸 817	suān 817	suan 817
818 south	南边 818	nánbian 818	nan-bian 818
819 space	空间 819	kōng jiān 819	kong jian 819
820 speak	讲 820	jiǎng 820	jeang 820

English		Simplified Chinese	Pinyin (with tone-accents)	Romanized transliteration
821	spice	香料 821	xiāng liào 821	shiang liaw 821
822	sponge	海绵 822	hǎi mián 822	hae mian 822
823	spoon	匙子 823	chízi 823	chyrtz 823
824	spring	春天 824	chūn tiān 824	chuen tian 824
825	stable	马棚 825	mǎ péng 825	maa perng 825
826	staircase	楼梯 826	lóu tī 826	lou ti 826
827	stamp (mail)	邮票 827	yóu piào 827	you piaw 827
828	stamp (seal)	图章 828	tú zhāng 828	twu jang 828
829	stand	站 829	zhàn 829	jann 829
830	star	星星 830	xīngxing 830	shing-shing 830
831	starch	糨糊 831	jiànghu 831	jiang-hwu 831
832	station	车站 832	chē zhàn 832	che jann 832
833	steal	偷 833	tōu 833	tou 833
834	steel	钢 834	gāng 834	gang 834
835	stick	棍子 835	gùnzi 835	guentz 835
836	sting	刺 836	cì 836	tsyh 836
837	stockings	长袜子 837	cháng wàzi 837	charng wahtz 837
838	stomach	胃 838	wèi 838	wey 838
839	stone	石头 839	shitou 839	shyr-tou 839
840	stop	停止 840	tíng zhǐ 840	tyng jyy 840

English	Simplified Chinese	Pinyin (with tone-accents)	Romanized transliteration
841 store	商店 841	shāng diàn 841	shang diann 841
842 storm	暴风雨 842	bào fēng yǔ 842	baw feng yeu 842
843 stove	暖炉 843	nuǎn lú 843	noan lu 843
844 straight	直 844	zhí 844	jyr 844
845 street	街道 845	jiē dào 845	jie daw 845
846 strong	强 846	qiáng 846	chyang 846
847 stubborn	顽固 847	wán gù 847	wan guh 847
848 sugar	糖 848	táng 848	tarng 848
849 summer	夏天 849	xià tiān 849	shiah tian 849
850 sun	太阳 850	tài yáng 850	tay yang 850
851 Sunday	星期天 851	xīng qī tiān 851	shing chi tian 851
852 surface	表面 852	biǎo miàn 852	beau miann 852
853 surprise	惊讶 853	jīng yà 853	jing yah 853
854 suspenders	吊裤带 854	diào kù dài 854	diaw kuh day 854
855 swallow	吞 855	tūn 855	tuen 855
856 sweet	甜 856	tián 856	tyan 856
857 swim	游泳 857	yóu yǒng 857	you yeong 857
858 switch	开关 858	kāi guān 858	kai guan 858
859 table	桌子 859	zhuōzi 859	juotz 859
860 tail	尾巴 860	wěiba 860	woei-ba 860

English	Simplified Chinese	Pinyin (with tone-accents)	Romanized transliteration
861 tailor	裁缝店 861	cáiféng diàn 861	tzair-feng diann 861
862 take	拿 862	ná 862	na 862
863 tall	高 863	gāo 863	gau 863
864 tame	驯服 864	xùn fú 864	shyun fwu 864
865 taste	味道 865	wèidao 865	wey-daw 865
866 tax	税 866	shuì 866	shuey 866
867 teacher	老师 867	lǎo shī 867	lao shy 867
868 tears	眼泪 868	yǎn lèi 868	yean ley 868
869 tedious	无聊 869	wú liáo 869	wu liau 869
870 ten	十 870	shí 870	shyr 870
871 tent	帐篷 871	zhàngpeng 871	janq-perng 871
872 test	考试 872	kǎo shì 872	kao shyh 872
873 thanks	谢谢 873	xièxie 873	shieh-shieh 873
874 thaw	解冻 874	jiě dòng 874	jiee donq 874
875 there	那里 875	nàli 875	nah-lii 875
876 thick	厚 876	hòu 876	how 876
877 thief	小偷 877	xiǎo tōu 877	sheau tou 877
878 thigh	大腿 878	dà tuǐ 878	dah toei 878
879 thin	薄 879	báo 879	baur 879
880 think	想 880	xiǎng 880	sheang 880

English	Simplified Chinese	Pinyin (with tone-accents)	Romanized transliteration
881 thirst	渴 881	kě 881	kee 881
882 thirteen	十三 882	shí sān 882	shyr san 882
883 thirty	三十 883	sān shí 883	san shyr 883
884 thousand	千 884	qiān 884	chian 884
885 thread	线 885	xiàn 885	shiann 885
886 three	三 886	sān 886	san 886
887 throat	喉咙 887	hóu lóng 887	hour long 887
888 throw	投 888	tóu 888	tour 888
889 thumb	拇指 889	mǔ zhǐ 889	muu jyy 889
890 thunder	雷声 890	léi shēng 890	lei sheng 890
891 Thursday	星期四 891	xīng qī sì 891	shing chi syh 891
892 ticket	票 892	piào 892	piaw 892
893 tide	潮 893	cháo 893	chaur 893
894 tie	领带 894	lǐng dài 894	liing day 894
895 time	时间 895	shí jiān 895	shyr jian 895
896 timetable	时间表 896	shí jiān biǎo 896	shyr jian beau 896
897 tin	锡 897	xī 897	shi 897
898 tip	小费 898	xiǎo fèi 898	sheau fey 898
899 tire	轮胎 899	lún tāi 899	luen tai 899
900 tired	累 900	lèi 900	ley 900

English	Simplified Chinese	Pinyin (with tone-accents)	Romanized transliteration
901 today	今天 901	jīn tiān 901	jin tian 901
902 toe	脚尖 902	jiǎo jiān 902	jeau jian 902
903 together	一起 903	yì qǐ 903	yih chii 903
904 toilet (WC)	厕所 904	cè suǒ 904	tseh suoo 904
905 tomorrow	明天 905	míng tiān 905	ming tian 905
906 tongue	舌头 906	shétou 906	sher-tou 906
907 tool	工具 907	gōng jù 907	gong jiuh 907
908 tooth	牙齿 908	yá chǐ 908	ya chyy 908
909 toothbrush	牙刷 909	yá shuā 909	ya shua 909
910 towel	毛巾 910	máo jīn 910	mau jin 910
911 town	镇 911	zhèn 911	jenn 911
912 town hall	市政厅 912	shì zhèng tīng 912	shyh jenq ting 912
913 toy	玩具 913	wán jù 913	wan jiuh 913
914 train	火车 914	huǒ chē 914	huoo che 914
915 transfer	搬 915	bān 915	ban 915
916 translate	翻译 916	fān yì 916	fan yih 916
917 transparent	透明 917	tòu míng 917	tow ming 917
918 travel	旅行 918	lǚ xíng 918	leu shyng 918
919 tree	树 919	shù 919	shuh 919
920 trouble	麻烦 920	máfan 920	ma-farn 920

English	Simplified Chinese	Pinyin (with tone-accents)	Romanized transliteration
921 trousers	裤子 921	kùzi 921	kuhtz 921
922 truth	真实 922	zhēn shí 922	jen shyr 922
923 try	试 923	shì 923	shyh 923
924 Tuesday	星期二 924	xīng qī èr 924	shing chi ell 924
925 turkey	火鸡 925	huǒ jī 925	huoo ji 925
926 turn	转 926	zhuǎn 926	juann 926
927 twelve	十二 927	shí èr 927	shyr ell 927
928 twenty	二十 928	èr shí 928	ell shyr 928
929 two	二 929	èr 929	ell 929
930 typewriter	打字机 930	dǎ zì jī 930	daa tzyh ji 930
931 ugly	难看 931	nán kàn 931	nan kann 931
932 umbrella	伞子 932	sǎnzi 932	saantz 932
933 uncle	伯父 933	bó fù 933	bor fuh 933
934 under	在下 934	zài xià 934	tzay shiah 934
935 underground (subway)	地下铁道 935	dì xià tiě dào 935	dih shiah tiee daw 935
936 understand	了解 936	liǎo jiě 936	leau jiee 936
937 underwear	内衣 937	nèi yī 937	ney i 937
938 until	到 938	dào 938	daw 938
939 upset	打翻 939	dǎ fān 939	daa fan 939
940 upstairs	楼上 940	lóu shàng 940	lou shanq 940

English	Simplified Chinese	Pinyin (with tone-accents)	Romanized transliteration
941 urgent	紧急 941	jǐn jí 941	jiin jyi 941
942 use	使用 942	shǐ yòng 942	shyy yonq 942
943 vacation	假期 943	jià qī 943	jiah chi 943
944 value	价值 944	jià zhí 944	jiah jyr 944
945 veal	犊肉 945	dú ròu 945	dwu row 945
946 vegetable	蔬菜 946	shū cài 946	shu tsay 946
947 velvet	天鹅绒 947	tiān é róng 947	tian er rong 947
948 very	很 948	hěn 948	heen 948
949 victim	被害者 949	bèi hài zhě 949	bey hay jee 949
950 view	眺望 950	tiào wàng 950	tiaw wang 950
951 village	村 951	cūn 951	tsuen 951
952 vinegar	醋 952	cù 952	tsuh 952
953 violation	违反 953	wéi fǎn 953	wei faan 953
954 visit	访问 954	fǎng wèn 954	faang wenn 954
955 voice	声 955	shēng 955	sheng 955
956 wages	工资 956	gōng zī 956	gong tzy 956
957 wait	等 957	děng 957	deeng 957
958 waiter	服务员 958	fú wù yuán 958	fwu wuh yuan 958
959 walk	走 959	zǒu 959	tzoou 959
960 wall	墙 960	qiáng 960	chyang 960

English	Simplified Chinese	Pinyin (with tone-accents)	Romanized transliteration
961 war	战争 961	zhàn zhēng 961	jann jeng 961
962 warm	暖和 962	nuǎnhuo 962	noan-huo 962
963 wash	洗 963	xǐ 963	shii 963
964 waste	垃圾 964	lā jī 964	lha ji 964
965 watch	表 965	biǎo 965	beau 965
966 water	水 966	shuǐ 966	shoei 966
967 way	道路 967	dào lù 967	daw luh 967
968 weather	天气 968	tiān qì 968	tian chih 968
969 wedding	婚礼 969	hūn lǐ 969	huen lii 969
970 Wednesday	星期三 970	xīng qī sān 970	shing chi san 970
971 week	星期 971	xīng qī 971	shing chi 971
972 weight	重量 972	zhòng liàng 972	jonq lianq 972
973 welcome	欢迎 973	huān yíng 973	huan yng 973
974 west	西边 974	xībian 974	shi-bian 974
975 wet	湿 975	shī 975	shy 975
976 wheel	车轮 976	chē lún 976	che luen 976
977 where?	哪里？977	nǎli? 977	naa-lii? 977
978 white	白 978	bái 978	bair 978
979 who?	谁？979	shuí? 979	shwei? 979
980 why?	为什么？980	wèi shénme? 980	wey shern-me? 980

English	Simplified Chinese	Pinyin (with tone-accents)	Romanized transliteration
981 widow	寡妇 981	guǎfu 981	goa-fuh 981
982 wind	风 982	fēng 982	feng 982
983 window	窗户 983	chuānghu 983	chuang-huh 983
984 wine	葡萄酒 984	pú táo jiǔ 984	pwu taur jeou 984
985 winter	冬天 985	dōng tiān 985	dong tian 985
986 witness	证人 986	zhèng rén 986	jenq ren 986
987 woman	妇女 987	fù nǚ 987	fuh neu 987
988 wood	木头 988	mùtou 988	muh-tou 988
989 wool	毛织物 989	máo zhī wù 989	mau jy wuh 989
990 word	词 990	cí 990	tsyr 990
991 work	工作 991	gōng zuò 991	gong tzuoh 991
992 world	世界 992	shì jiè 992	shyh jieh 992
993 write	写 993	xiě 993	shiee 993
994 wrong	错误 994	cuò wù 994	tsuoh wuh 994
995 year	年 995	nián 995	nian 995
996 yellow	黄 996	huáng 996	hwang 996
997 yes	是 997	shì 997	shyh 997
998 yesterday	昨天 998	zuó tiān 998	tzwo tian 998
999 young	年轻 999	nián qīng 999	nian ching 999
1000 zero	零 1000	líng 1000	ling 1000

Simplified Chinese	Pinyin (with tone-accents)	Romanized transliteration	English
1 画			
一 630	yī 630	i 630	630 one
一月 484	yí yuè 484	yi yueh 484	484 January
一个 668	yíge 668	yi-geh 668	668 piece
一半 431	yí bàn 431	yi bann 431	431 half
一点 347	yì diǎn 347	yih dean 347	347 few
一起 903	yì qǐ 903	yih chii 903	903 together
2 画			
二 929	èr 929	ell 929	929 two
二十 928	èr shí 928	ell shyr 928	928 twenty
二月 344	èr yuè 344	ell yueh 344	344 February
七 772	qī 772	chi 772	772 seven
七十 774	qī shí 774	chi shyr 774	774 seventy
七月 488	qī yuè 488	chi yueh 488	488 July
八 313	bā 313	ba 313	313 eight
八十 315	bā shí 315	ba shyr 315	315 eighty
八月 48	bá yuè 48	bar yueh 48	48 August
九 608	jiǔ 608	jeou 608	608 nine
九十 610	jiǔ shí 610	jeou shyr 610	610 ninety
九月 770	jiǔ yuè 770	jeou yueh 770	770 September
十 870	shí 870	shyr 870	870 ten
十一 318	shí yī 318	shyr i 318	318 eleven

Simplified Chinese	Pinyin (with tone-accents)	Romanized transliteration	English
十二 927	shí èr 927	shyr ell 927	twelve
十三 882	shí sān 882	shyr san 882	thirteen
十四 375	shí sì 375	shyr syh 375	fourteen
十五 348	shí wǔ 348	shyr wuu 348	fifteen
十六 797	shí liù 797	shyr liow 797	sixteen
十七 773	shí qī 773	shyr chi 773	seventeen
十八 314	shí bā 314	shyr ba 314	eighteen
十九 609	shí jiǔ 609	shyr jeou 609	nineteen
十月 626	shí yuè 626	shyr yueh 626	October
十一月 617	shí yī yuè 617	shyr i yueh 617	November
十二月 255	shí èr yuè 255	shyr ell yueh 255	December
丁香花 524	dīng xiāng huā 524	ding shiang hua 524	lilac
了解 936	liǎo jiě 936	leau jiee 936	understand
人造 45	rén zào 45	ren tzaw 45	artificial
入口 321	rù kǒu 321	ruh koou 321	entrance
儿子 813	érzi 813	erlz 813	son
义务 302	yì wù 302	yih wuh 302	duty
…之间 99	…zhī jiān 99	…jy jian 99	between
三 886	sān 886	san 886	three
三十 883	sān shí 883	san shyr 883	thirty

3 画

Simplified Chinese	Pinyin (with tone-accents)	Romanized transliteration	English
三月 550	sān yuè 550	san yueh 550	550 March
干净 195	gān jìng 195	gan jinq 195	195 clean
干酪 182	gān lào 182	gan law 182	182 cheese
干燥 299	gān zào 299	gan tzaw 299	299 dry
下午 13	xià wǔ 13	shiah wuu 13	13 afternoon
下巴 189	xiàba 189	shiah-ba 189	189 chin
山羊 410	shān yáng 410	shan yang 410	410 goat
上油 536	shàng yóu 536	shanq you 536	536 lubricating
上帝 411	shàng dì 411	shanq dih 411	411 God
丈夫 468	zhàngfu 468	janq-fu 468	468 husband
飞机 20	fēi jī 20	fei ji 20	20 airplane
乞丐 87	qǐ gài 87	chii gay 87	87 beggar
习惯 427	xí guàn 427	shyi guann 427	427 habit
也 26	yě 26	yee 26	26 also
也许 556	yě xǔ 556	yee sheu 556	556 maybe
千 884	qiān 884	chian 884	884 thousand
叉子 371	chāzi 371	chatz 371	371 fork
门 285	mén 285	men 285	285 door
工厂 336	gōng chǎng 336	gong chaang 336	336 factory
工作 991	gōng zuò 991	gong tzuoh 991	991 work

Simplified Chinese	Pinyin (with tone-accents)	Romanized transliteration	English
工具 907	gōng jù 907	gong jiuh 907	907 tool
工资 956	gōng zī 956	gong tzy 956	956 wages
土豆 695	tǔ dòu 695	tuu dow 695	695 potato
大 502	dà 502	dah 502	502 large
大麦 67	dà mài 67	dah may 67	67 barley
大理石 549	dà lǐ shí 549	dah lii shyr 549	549 marble
大蒜 397	dà suàn 397	dah suann 397	397 garlic
大腿 878	dà tuǐ 878	dah toei 878	878 thigh
小 805	xiǎo 805	sheau 805	805 small
小刀子 496	xiǎo dāozi 496	sheau dautz 496	496 knife
小心 161	xiǎo xīn 161	sheau shin 161	161 careful
小床 238	xiǎo chuáng 238	sheau chwang 238	238 crib
小时 461	xiǎo shí 461	sheau shyr 461	461 hour
小姐 569	xiǎo jiě 569	sheau jiee 569	569 Miss
小孩 187	xiǎo hái 187	sheau hair 187	187 child
小费 898	xiǎo fèi 898	sheau fey 898	898 tip
小偷 877	xiǎo tōu 877	sheau tou 877	877 thief
口袋 685	kǒudai 685	koou-day 685	685 pocket
山 579	shān 579	shan 579	579 mountain
已经 25	yǐjing 25	yii-jing 25	25 already

Simplified Chinese	Pinyin (with tone-accents)	Romanized transliteration	English
子弹 142	zǐ dàn 142	tzyy dann 142	142 bullet
女儿 250	nǚ ér 250	neu erl 250	250 daughter
女仆 542	nǚ pú 542	neu pwu 542	542 maid
女性 345	nǚ xìng 345	neu shing 345	345 female
女孩子 403	nǚ háizi 403	neu hairtz 403	403 girl
马 457	mǎ 457	maa 457	457 horse
马棚 825	mǎ péng 825	maa perng 825	825 stable
为什么 980	wèi shénme? 980	wey shernme? 980	980 why?
4 画 开 293	kāi 293	kai 293	293 drive
开关 858	kāi guān 858	kai guan 858	858 switch
开始 88	kāi shǐ 88	kai shyy 88	88 begin
开的 633	kāide 633	kai-de 633	633 open
开塞钻 221	kāi sāi zuàn 221	kai sai tzuann 221	221 corkscrew
无花果 350	wú huā guǒ 350	wu hua guoo 350	350 fig
无聊 869	wú liáo 869	wu liau 869	869 tedious
天 251	tiān 251	tian 251	251 day
天气 968	tiān qì 968	tian chih 968	968 weather
天空 801	tiān kōng 801	tian kong 801	801 sky
天鹅绒 947	tiān é róng 947	tian er rong 947	947 velvet
夫人 585	fū rén 585	fu ren 585	585 Mrs (addressing)

Simplified Chinese	Pinyin (with tone-accents)	Romanized transliteration	English
五 357	wǔ 357	wuu 357	357 five
五十 349	wǔ shí 349	wuu shyr 349	349 fifty
五月 555	wǔ yuè 555	wuu yueh 555	555 May
六 796	liù 796	liow 796	796 six
六十 798	liù shí 798	liow shyr 798	798 sixty
六月 489	liù yuè 489	liow yueh 489	489 June
不 611	bù 611	buh 611	611 no
不同 269	bù tóng 269	buh torng 269	269 different
牙医 260	yá yī 260	ya i 260	260 dentist
牙刷 909	yá shuā 909	ya shua 909	909 toothbrush
牙齿 908	yá chǐ 908	ya chyy 908	908 tooth
互相 591	hù xiāng 591	huh shiang 591	591 mutual
中午 614	zhōng wǔ 614	jong wuu 614	614 noon
中间 566	zhōng jiān 566	jong jian 566	566 middle
书 120	shū 120	shu 120	120 book
长 532	cháng 532	charng 532	532 long
长沙发椅 226	cháng shā fā yǐ 226	charng sha fa yii 226	226 couch
长袜子 837	cháng wàzi 837	charng wahtz 837	837 stockings
午饭 538	wǔ fàn 538	wuu fann 538	538 lunch
以后 12	yǐ hòu 12	yii how 12	12 after

Simplified Chinese	Pinyin (with tone-accents)	Romanized transliteration	English
内衣 937	nèi yī 937	ney i 937	937 underwear
云彩 201	yún cǎi 201	yun tsae 201	201 cloud
认真 771	rèn zhēn 771	renn jen 771	771 serious
公牛 638	gōng niú 638	gong niou 638	638 ox
公寓 35	gōng yù 35	gong yuh 35	35 apartment
公路 453	gōng lù 453	gong luh 453	453 highway
分隔间 212	fēn gé jiān 212	fen ger jian 212	212 compartment
今天 901	jīn tiān 901	jin tian 901	901 today
从 385	cóng 385	tsorng 385	385 from
风 982	fēng 982	feng 982	982 wind
切 246	qiē 246	chie 246	246 cut
办事处 627	bàn shì chù 627	bann shyh chuh 627	627 office
劝告 10	quàn gào 10	chiuann gaw 10	10 advice
艺术 44	yì shù 44	yih shuh 44	44 art
太阳 850	tài yáng 850	tay yang 850	850 sun
孔 454	kǒng 454	koong 454	454 hole
文件 281	wén jiàn 281	wen jiann 281	281 document
方向 273	fāng xiàng 273	fang shiang 273	273 direction
火 354	huǒ 354	huoo 354	354 fire
火车 914	huǒ chē 914	huoo che 914	914 train

Simplified Chinese		Pinyin (with tone-accents)		Romanized transliteration		English	
火鸡	925	huǒ jī 925		huoo ji 925		925	turkey
火柴	553	huǒ chái 553		huoo chair 553		553	match
火腿	432	huǒ tuǐ 432		huoo toei 432		432	ham
心脏	447	xīn zàng 447		shin tzang 447		447	heart
木头	988	mùtou 988		muh-tou 988		988	wood
车	159	chē 159		che 159		159	car
车轮	976	chē lún 976		che luen 976		976	wheel
车站	832	chē zhàn 832		che jann 832		832	station
车费	339	chē fèi 339		che fey 339		339	fare
比赛	394	bǐ sài 394		bii say 394		394	game
水	966	shuǐ 966		shoei 966		966	water
水手	747	shuǐ shǒu 747		shoei shoou 747		747	sailor
水果	387	shuǐ guǒ 387		shoei guoo 387		387	fruit
父母	648	fù mǔ 648		fuh muu 648		648	parents
父亲	342	fù qīn 342		fuh chin 342		342	father
牛奶	567	niú nǎi 567		niou nae 567		567	milk
牛肉	85	niú ròu 85		niou row 85		85	beef
手	434	shǒu 434		shoou 434		434	hand
手巾	435	shǒu jīn 435		shoou jin 435		435	handkerchief
手指	352	shǒu zhǐ 352		shoou jyy 352		352	finger

Simplified Chinese	Pinyin (with tone-accents)	Romanized transliteration	English
手套 407	shǒu tào 407	shoou taw 407	407 glove
手提式 690	shǒu tí shì 690	shoou tyi shyh 690	690 portable
手镯 125	shǒu zhuó 125	shoou jwo 125	125 bracelet
毛巾 910	máo jīn 910	mau jin 910	910 towel
毛织物 989	máo zhī wù 989	mau jy wuh 989	989 wool
毛毯 109	máo tǎn 109	mau taan 109	109 blanket
气息 132	qì xī 132	chih shi 132	132 breath
月 573	yuè 573	yueh 573	573 month
月亮 574	yuèliang 574	yueh-liang 574	574 moon
头 444	tóu 444	tour 444	444 head
头发 429	tóu fà 429	tour faa 429	429 hair
半旧 763	bàn jiù 763	bann jiow 763	763 second-hand
必要 599	bì yào 599	bih yaw 599	599 need
平 358	píng 358	pyng 358	358 flat
未喝醉的 811	wèi hē zuìde 811	wey he tzuey-de 811	811 sober
正面 386	zhèng miàn 386	jenq miann 386	386 front
正确 223	zhèng què 223	jenq chiueh 223	223 correct
世纪 175	shì jì 175	shyh jih 175	175 century
世界 992	shì jiè 992	shyh jieh 992	992 world
可靠 765	kě kào 765	kee kaw 765	765 secure

5 画

Simplified Chinese	Pinyin (with tone-accents)	Romanized transliteration	English
左边 514	zuǒbian 514	tzuoo-bian 514	514 left
右边 728	yòubian 728	yow-bian 728	728 right
东边 308	dōng biān 308	dong bian 308	308 east
四 374	sì 374	syh 374	374 four
四十 372	sì shí 372	syh shyr 372	372 forty
四月 41	sì yuè 41	syh yueh 41	41 April
四分之一 703	sì fēn zhī yī 703	syh fen jy i 703	703 quarter
北边 615	běi biān 615	beei bian 615	615 north
电灯泡 522	diàn dēng pào 522	diann deng paw 522	522 light bulb
电梯 317	diàn tī 317	diann ti 317	317 elevator (lift)
电影 583	diàn yǐng 583	diann yiing 583	583 movie
出口 327	chū kǒu 327	chu koou 327	327 exit
出发 261	chū fā 261	chu fa 261	261 departure
出汗 663	chū hàn 663	chu hann 663	663 perspire
出现 36	chū xiàn 36	chu shiann 36	36 appear
生 712	shēng 712	sheng 712	712 raw
生日 104	shēng rì 104	sheng ryh 104	104 birthday
生气 30	shēng qì 30	sheng chih 30	30 angry
生命 519	shēng mìng 519	sheng ming 519	519 life
生锈的 743	shēng xiùde 743	sheng shiow-de 743	743 rusty

Simplified Chinese	Pinyin (with tone-accents)	Romanized transliteration	English
冬天 985	dōng tiān 985	dong tian 985	985 winter
发现 351	fā xiàn 351	fa shiann 351	351 find
发明 479	fā míng 479	fa ming 479	479 invention
市长 557	shì zhǎng 557	shyh jaang 557	557 mayor
市民 194	shì mín 194	shyh min 194	194 citizen
市场 551	shì chǎng 551	shyh chaang 551	551 market
市政厅 912	shì zhèng tīng 912	shyh jeng ting 912	912 town hall
写 993	xiě 993	shiee 993	993 write
占 625	zhàn 625	jann 625	625 occupy
他 443	tā 443	ta 443	443 he
包 59	bāo 59	bau 59	59 bag
包裹 647	bāo guǒ 647	bau guoo 647	647 parcel
圣诞节 190	shèng dàn jié 190	sheng dann jye 190	190 Christmas
对 15	duì 15	duey 15	15 against
对 642	duì 642	duey 642	642 pair
印刷 698	yìn shuā 698	yinn shua 698	698 printing
闪电 523	shǎn diàn 523	shaan diann 523	523 lightning
边界 121	biān jiè 121	bian jieh 121	121 border
打字机 930	dǎ zì jī 930	daa tzyh ji 930	930 typewriter
打猎 467	dǎ liè 467	daa lieh 467	467 hunt

Simplified Chinese	Pinyin (with tone-accents)	Romanized transliteration	English
打赌 97	dǎ dǔ 97	daa duu 97	97 bet
打翻 939	dǎ fān 939	daa fan 939	939 upset
扑克 679	pū kè 679	pu keh 679	679 playing card
去 409	qù 409	chiuh 409	409 go
节日 455	jié rì 455	jye ryh 455	455 holiday
叶子 510	yèzi 510	yehtz 510	510 leaf
只 632	zhǐ 632	jyy 632	632 only
叫 153	jiào 153	jiaw 153	153 call
司机 294	sī jī 294	sy ji 294	294 driver
外 637	wài 637	way 637	637 outside
外衣 203	wài yī 203	way i 203	203 coat
外国 368	wài guó 368	way gwo 368	368 foreign
犯罪 239	fàn zuì 239	fann tzuey 239	239 crime
奶脂 237	nǎi zhī 237	nae jy 237	237 cream
丝绸 791	sī chóu 791	sy chour 791	791 silk
礼物 402	lǐ wù 402	lii wuh 402	402 gift
玉米 222	yù mǐ 222	yuh mii 222	222 corn (maize)
旧 629	jiù 629	jiow 629	629 old
母牛 232	mǔ niú 232	muu niou 232	232 cow
母亲 578	mǔqin 578	muu-chin 578	578 mother

Simplified Chinese	Pinyin (with tone-accents)	Romanized transliteration	English
石头 839	shítou 839	shyr-tou 839	839 stone
龙虾 530	lóng xiā 530	long shia 530	530 lobster
目的 18	mù dì 18	muh dih 18	18 aim
白 978	bái 978	bair 978	978 white
皮外衣 390	pí wài yī 390	pyi way i 390	390 fur coat
皮肤 799	pí fū 799	pyi fu 799	799 skin
皮革 512	pí gé 512	pyi ger 512	512 leather
6 闽 再 14	zài 14	tzay 14	14 again
再见 414	zài jiàn 414	tzay jiann 414	414 goodbye
亚麻布 525	yà má bù 525	yah ma buh 525	525 linen
考试 872	kǎo shì 872	kao shyh 872	872 test
百 465	bǎi 465	bae 465	465 hundred
有 442	yǒu 442	yeou 442	442 have
有毛病 257	yǒu máo bìng 257	yeou mau bing 257	257 defective
有病 787	yǒu bìng 787	yeou bing 787	787 sick
有效 52	yǒu xiào 52	yeou shiaw 52	52 available
有罪 426	yǒu zuì 426	yeou tzuey 426	426 guilty
死 253	sǐ 253	syy 253	253 death
肉 559	ròu 559	row 559	559 meat
肉汁 419	ròu zhī 419	row jy 419	419 gravy

Simplified Chinese	Pinyin (with tone-accents)	Romanized transliteration	English
肉店 145	ròu diàn 145	row diann 145	145 butcher
关 199	guān 199	guan 199	199 close
关系 215	guānxi 215	guan-shih 215	215 connection
年 995	nián 995	nian 995	995 year
年岁 16	nián suì 16	nian suey 16	16 age
年轻 999	nián qīng 999	nian ching 999	999 young
向下 287	xiàng xià 287	shiang shiah 287	287 down
向后 57	xiàng hòu 57	shiang how 57	57 backward
危险 248	wēi xiǎn 248	uei shean 248	248 danger
危险 732	wēi xiǎn 732	uei shean 732	732 risk
买 149	mǎi 149	mae 149	149 buy
买卖 144	mǎi mài 144	mae may 144	144 business
交易所 324	jiāo yì suǒ 324	jiau yih suoo 324	324 exchange
交钱 654	jiāo qián 654	jiau chyan 654	654 pay
充满 388	chōng mǎn 388	chong maan 388	388 full
决不 604	jué bù 604	jyue buh 604	604 never
冰 469	bīng 469	bing 469	469 ice
冰淇淋 470	bīng qí lín 470	bing chyi lin 470	470 ice cream
农民 658	nóng mín 658	nong min 658	658 peasant
访问 954	fǎng wèn 954	faang wenn 954	954 visit

Simplified Chinese	Pinyin (with tone-accents)	Romanized transliteration	English
讲 820	jiǎng 820	jeang 820	820 speak
许可 662	xǔ kě 662	sheu kee 662	662 permission
许多 586	xǔ duō 586	sheu duo 586	586 much
网 603	wǎng 603	woang 603	603 net (fishing)
同意 17	tóng yì 17	torng yih 17	17 agree
伞子 932	sǎnzi 932	saantz 932	932 umbrella
全部 22	quán bù 22	chyuan buh 22	22 all
会员 562	huì yuán 562	huey yuan 562	562 member
传染性 217	chuán rǎn xìng 217	chwan raan shing 217	217 contagious
价钱 697	jiàqian 697	jiah-chyan 697	697 price
价值 944	jià zhí 944	jiah jyr 944	944 value
光 521	guāng 521	guang 521	521 light
先生 584	xiānsheng 584	shiang-sheng 584	584 Mr (addressing)
收获 439	shōu huò 439	shou huoh 439	439 harvest
收据 715	shōu jù 715	shou jiuh 715	715 receipt
欢乐 565	huān lè 565	huan leh 565	565 merry
欢迎 973	huān yíng 973	huan yng 973	973 welcome
那里 875	nàli 875	nah-lii 875	875 there
动 582	dòng 582	donq 582	582 move
动物 31	dòng wù 31	dong wuh 31	31 animal

Simplified Chinese	Pinyin (with tone-accents)	Romanized transliteration	English
汤 816	tāng 816	tang 816	816 soup
安全 746	ān quán 746	an chyuan 746	746 safety
安全带 520	ān quán dài 520	an chyuan day 520	520 life belt
安静 706	ān jìng 706	an jing 706	706 quiet
安慰 211	ān wèi 211	an wey 211	211 comfort
问 46	wèn 46	wenn 46	46 ask
问题 704	wèn tí 704	wenn tyi 704	704 question
迅速 705	xùn sù 705	shiunn suh 705	705 quick
导管 675	dǎo guǎn 675	dao goan 675	675 pipe (tube)
扣子 148	kòuzi 148	kowtz 148	148 button
扫帚 137	sàozhou 137	saw-joou 137	137 broom
在下 94	zài xià 94	tzay shiah 94	94 below
在下 934	zài xià 934	tzay shiah 934	934 under
在后 90	zài hòu 90	tzay how 90	90 behind
地下室 69	dì xià shì 69	dih shiah shyh 69	69 basement
地下室 173	dì xià shì 173	dih shiah shyh 173	173 cellar
地下铁道 935	dì xià tiě dào 935	dih shiah tiee daw 935	935 underground (subway)
地址 9	dì zhǐ 9	dih jyy 9	9 address
地图 548	dì tú 548	dih twu 548	548 map
地板 360	dì bǎn 360	dih baan 360	360 floor

Simplified Chinese	Pinyin (with tone-accents)	Romanized transliteration	English
地球 306	dì qiú 306	dih chyou 306	306 earth
地毯 164	dì tǎn 164	dih taan 164	164 carpet
地震 307	dì zhèn 307	dih jenn 307	307 earthquake
吊袜带 398	diào wà dài 398	diaw wah day 398	393 garter
吊裤带 854	diào kù dài 854	diaw kuh day 854	854 suspenders
吃 310	chī 310	chy 310	310 eat
因为 81	yīn wèi 81	in wey 81	81 because
回 725	huí 725	hwei 725	725 return
回答 33	huí dá 33	hwei dar 33	33 answer
行为 89	xíng wéi 89	shyng wei 89	89 behavior
行李 60	xíng lǐ 60	shyng lii 60	60 baggage
名字 594	míngzi 594	mingtz 594	594 name
多少钱？ 464	duō shǎo qián? 464	duo shao chyan? 464	464 how much?
存局候领的邮件 400	cún jú hòu lǐngdì yóu jiàn 400	tswen jyu how liing-dih you jiann 400	400 general delivery
妇女 987	fù nǚ 987	fuh neu 987	987 woman
她 778	tā 778	ta 778	778 she
好 23	hǎo 23	hao 23	23 all right
好 413	hǎo 413	hao 413	413 good
红 716	hóng 716	horng 716	716 red
约定 39	yuē dìng 39	iue ding 39	39 appointment

Simplified Chinese	Pinyin (with tone-accents)	Romanized transliteration	English
驯服 864	xún fú 864	shyun fwu 864	tame
灰色 421	huī sè 421	huei seh 421	grey
灰尘 301	huī chén 301	huei chern 301	dust
杂志 540	zá zhì 540	tzar jyh 540	magazine
机会 178	jī huì 178	ji huey 178	chance
机场 21	jī chǎng 21	ji chaang 21	airport
权威 50	quán wēi 50	chyuan uei 50	authority
划分 279	huà fēn 279	huah fen 279	divide
成长 422	chéng zhǎng 422	cherng jaang 422	growing
成熟 730	chéng shú 730	cherng shwu 730	ripe
早 304	zǎo 304	tzao 304	early
早饭 130	zǎo fàn 130	tzao fann 130	breakfast
早晨 576	zǎo chén 576	tzao chern 576	morning
肌肉 587	jī ròu 587	ji row 587	muscle
鸟 102	niǎo 102	neau 102	bird
衣服 200	yī fú 200	i fwu 200	clothing
衣领 207	yī lǐng 207	i liing 207	collar
羊 779	yáng 779	yang 779	sheep
羊羔 500	yáng gāo 500	yang gau 500	lamb
老师 867	lǎo shī 867	lao shy 867	teacher

Simplified Chinese	Pinyin (with tone-accents)	Romanized transliteration	English
老鼠 711	lǎo shǔ 711	lao shuu 711	rat
耳朵 303	ěrduo 303	eel-duoo 303	ear
耳环 305	ěr huán 305	eel hwan 305	earring
西边 974	xībian 974	shi-bian 974	west
页 639	yè 639	yeh 639	page
舌头 906	shétou 906	sher-tou 906	tongue
自由 379	zì yóu 379	tzyh you 379	free
自行车 100	zì xíng chē 100	tzyh shyng che 100	bicycle
血 113	xuè 113	shiueh 113	blood
7 画			
来 210	lái 210	lai 210	come
更多 575	gèng duō 575	genq duo 575	more
证人 986	zhèng rén 986	jenq ren 986	witness
词 990	cí 990	tsyr 990	word
医生 666	yī shēng 666	i sheng 666	physician
医院 459	yī yuàn 459	i yuann 459	hospital
别针 672	bié zhēn 672	bye jen 672	pin
伯父 933	bó fù 933	bor fuh 933	uncle
你好吗? 463	nǐ hǎoma? 463	nii hao-ma? 463	how are you?
鸡 186	jī 186	ji 186	chicken
鸡蛋 312	jī dàn 312	ji dann 312	egg

Simplified Chinese	Pinyin (with tone-accents)	Romanized transliteration	English
邮件 543	yóu jiàn 543	you jiann 543	543 mail
邮局 693	yóu jú 693	you jyu 693	693 post office
邮票 827	yóu piào 827	you piaw 827	827 stamp (mail)
邻居 602	lín jū 602	lin jiu 602	602 neighbor
男人 547	nán rén 547	nan ren 547	547 man
男性 545	nán xìng 545	nan shinq 545	545 male
男孩子 124	nán háizi 124	nan hairtz 124	124 boy
努力 311	nǔ lì 311	nuu lih 311	311 effort
汽油 399	qì yóu 399	chih you 399	399 gasoline (petrol)
沙子 750	shāzi 750	shatz 750	750 sand
沙漠 262	shā mò 262	sha moh 262	262 desert
怀疑 286	huái yí 286	hwai yi 286	286 doubt
快 340	kuài 340	kuay 340	340 fast
快乐 682	kuài lè 682	kuay leh 682	682 pleasure
床 82	chuáng 82	chwang 82	82 bed
床单 780	chuáng dān 780	chwang dan 780	780 sheets
这里 451	zhè lǐ 451	jeh lii 451	451 here
远 338	yuǎn 338	yeuan 338	338 far
违反 953	wéi fǎn 953	wei faan 953	953 violation
违法 471	wéi fǎ 471	wei fa 471	471 illegal

Simplified Chinese	Pinyin (with tone-accents)	Romanized transliteration	English
运气 537	yùnqi 537	yunn-chih 537	537 luck
连衣裙 291	lián yī qún 291	lian i chiun 291	291 dress
近 596	jìn 596	jinn 596	596 near
坟地 174	fén dì 174	fern dih 174	174 cemetery
护士 620	hùshi 620	huh-shyh 620	620 nurse
坏 58	huài 58	huay 58	58 bad
坚果 621	jiān guǒ 621	jian guoo 621	621 nut
坐 795	zuò 795	tzouh 795	795 sit
抓住 169	zhuā zhù 169	jua juh 169	169 catch
投 888	tóu 888	tour 888	888 throw
报纸 606	bào zhǐ 606	baw jyy 606	606 newspaper
声 955	shēng 955	sheng 955	955 voice
芦笋 47	lú sǔn 47	lu soen 47	47 asparagus
芥黄 589	jiè huáng 589	jieh hwang 589	589 mustard
苍白 643	cāng bái 643	tsang bair 643	643 pale
苍蝇 363	cāng yíng 363	tsang yng 363	363 fly
花 362	huā 362	hua 362	362 flower
花边 497	huā biān 497	hua bian 497	497 lace
吞 855	tūn 855	tuen 855	855 swallow
听 446	tīng 446	ting 446	446 hear

Simplified Chinese	Pinyin (with tone-accents)	Romanized transliteration	English
围巾 754	wéi jīn 754	wei jin 754	754 scarf
帐篷 871	zhàngpeng 871	janq-perng 871	871 tent
饭 558	fàn 558	fann 558	558 meal
尿布 266	niào bù 266	niaw buh 266	266 diaper (baby's napkin)
尾巴 860	wěiba 860	woei-ba 860	860 tail
弟兄 138	dì xiōng 138	dih shiong 138	138 brother
纸 645	zhǐ 645	jyy 645	645 paper
纸板 160	zhǐ bǎn 160	jyy baan 160	160 cardboard
驴 284	lǘ 284	liu 284	284 donkey
忘记 370	wàng jì 370	wang jih 370	370 forget
忍耐 653	rěn nài 653	reen nay 653	653 patience
村 951	cūn 951	tsuen 951	951 village
杏 40	xìng 40	shinq 40	40 apricot
条件 214	tiáo jiàn 214	tyau jiann 214	214 condition
极端 332	jí duān 332	jyi duan 332	332 extreme
李子 684	lǐzi 684	liitz 684	684 plum
戒指 729	jièzhi 729	jieh-jyy 729	729 ring
步枪 727	bù qiāng 727	buh chiang 727	727 rifle
时间 895	shí jiān 895	shyr jian 895	895 time
时间表 896	shí jiān biǎo 896	shyr jian beau 896	896 timetable

Simplified Chinese	Pinyin (with tone-accents)	Romanized transliteration	English
财产 701	cái chǎn 701	tsair chaan 701	701 property
肝脏 529	gān zàng 529	gan tzanq 529	529 liver
肚子 93	dùzi 93	duhtz 93	93 belly
肘 316	zhǒu 316	joou 316	316 elbow
穷 688	qióng 688	chyong 688	688 poor
针 600	zhēn 600	jen 600	600 needle
钉子 592	dīngzi 592	dingtz 592	592 nail
利息 477	lì xī 477	lih shi 477	477 interest
秃 63	tū 63	tu 63	63 bald
走 959	zǒu 959	tzoou 959	959 walk
赤裸裸 593	chì luǒ luǒ 593	chyh luoo luoo 593	593 naked
豆子 77	dòuzi 77	dowtz 77	77 bean
身体 117	shēn tǐ 117	shen tii 117	117 body
表 965	biǎo 965	beau 965	965 watch
表面 852	biǎo miàn 852	beau miann 852	852 surface
事件 11	shì jiàn 11	shyh jiann 11	11 affair
事故 5	shì gù 5	shyh guh 5	5 accident
画 667	huà 667	huah 667	667 picture
画框 378	huà kuàng 378	huah kuanq 378	378 frame
其他 636	qí tā 636	chyi ta 636	636 other

8 画

Simplified Chinese	Pinyin (with tone-accents)	Romanized transliteration	English
果酱 483	guǒ jiàng 483	guoo jianq 483	483 jam (marmalade)
变化 179	biàn huà 179	biann huah 179	179 change
试 923	shì 923	shyh 923	923 try
直 844	zhí 844	jyr 844	844 straight
卖 768	mài 768	may 768	768 sell
厕所 904	cè suǒ 904	tseh suoo 904	904 toilet (WC)
刺 836	cì 836	tsyh 836	836 sting
到 938	dào 938	daw 938	938 until
到达 43	dào dá 43	daw dar 43	43 arrival
制动器 127	zhì dòng qì 127	jyh donq chih 127	127 brake
刮脸 777	guā liǎn 777	gua lean 777	777 shave
刮脸刀 713	guā liǎn dāo 713	gua lean dau 713	713 razor
刷子 140	shuāzi 140	shuatz 140	140 brush
单身汉 55	dān shēn hàn 55	dan shen hann 55	55 bachelor
使用 942	shǐ yòng 942	shyy yonq 942	942 use
河 733	hé 733	her 733	733 river
油 628	yóu 628	you 628	628 oil
油炸鱼 382	yóu zhá yú 382	you jar yu 382	382 fried fish
怕羞 70	pà xiū 70	pah shiou 70	70 bashful
宝石 486	bǎo shí 486	bao shyr 486	486 jewel

Simplified Chinese	Pinyin (with tone-accents)	Romanized transliteration	English
空 319	kōng 319	kong 319	319 empty
空气 19	kōng qì 19	kong chih 19	19 air
空间 819	kōng jiān 819	kong jian 819	819 space
闹肚子 267	nào dùzi 267	naw duhtz 267	267 diarrhea
诞生 103	dàn shēng 103	dann sheng 103	103 birth
拇指 889	mǔ zhǐ 889	muu jyy 889	889 thumb
垃圾 395	lā jī 395	lha ji 395	395 garbage
垃圾 964	lā jī 964	lha ji 964	964 waste
苹果 38	píng guǒ 38	pyng guoo 38	38 apple
苹果酒 192	píng guǒ jiǔ 192	pyng guoo jeou 192	192 cider
苦 105	kǔ 105	kuu 105	105 bitter
味道 865	wèidao 865	wey-daw 865	865 taste
和 29	hé 29	her 29	29 and
国外 2	guó wài 2	gwo way 2	2 abroad
国家 229	guó jiā 229	gwo jia 229	229 country
图章 828	tú zhāng 828	twu jang 828	828 stamp (seal)
狐狸 376	húli 376	hwu-li 376	376 fox
狗 282	gǒu 282	goou 282	282 dog
学习 511	xué xí 511	shyue shyi 511	511 learn
学校 755	xué xiào 755	shyue shiaw 755	755 school

Simplified Chinese	Pinyin (with tone-accents)	Romanized transliteration	English
姑母 49	gū mǔ 49	gu muu 49	49 aunt
姐妹 794	jiě mèi 794	jiee mey 794	794 sister
线 885	xiàn 885	shiann 885	885 thread
经常 28	jīng cháng 28	jing charng 28	28 always
炊事员 218	chuī shì yuán 218	chuei shyh yuan 218	218 cook
炒鸡蛋 758	chǎo jī dàn 758	chao ji dann 758	758 scrambled eggs
房子 462	fángzi 462	farngtz 462	462 house
房租 722	fáng zū 722	farng tzu 722	722 rent
肩膀 784	jiān bǎng 784	jian baang 784	784 shoulder
肾脏 491	shèn zàng 491	shenn tzang 491	491 kidney
玩 678	wán 678	wan 678	678 play
玩具 913	wán jù 913	wan jiuh 913	913 toy
玩偶 283	wán ǒu 283	wan oou 283	283 doll
现在 618	xiàn zài 618	shiann tzay 618	618 now
现款 167	xiàn kuǎn 167	shiann koan 167	167 cash
枕头 671	zhěntou 671	jeen-tou 671	671 pillow
杯子 243	bēizi 243	beitz 243	243 cup
松树 673	sōng shù 673	song shuh 673	673 pine tree
或者 634	huò zhě 634	huoh jee 634	634 or
转 926	zhuàn 926	juann 926	926 turn

Simplified Chinese	Pinyin (with tone-accents)	Romanized transliteration	English
轮胎 899	lún tāi 899	luen tai 899	899 tire
软 812	ruǎn 812	roan 812	812 soft
软线 220	ruǎn xiàn 220	roan shiann 220	220 cord
昆虫 475	kūn chóng 475	kuen chorng 475	475 insect
明天 905	míng tiān 905	ming tian 905	905 tomorrow
明信片 692	míng xìn piàn 692	ming shinn piann 692	692 postcard
货币 572	huò bì 572	huoh bih 572	572 money
货物 162	huò wù 162	huoh wuh 162	162 cargo
帐单 101	zhàng dān 101	janq dan 101	101 bill
放松 719	fàng sōng 719	fanq song 719	719 relax
牧师 197	mù shī 197	muh shy 197	197 clergy
爬 235	pá 235	par 235	235 crawl
朋友 383	péng yǒu 383	perng yeou 383	383 friend
肥皂 810	féi zào 810	feir tzaw 810	810 soap
服务员 958	fú wù yuán 958	fwu wuh yuan 958	958 waiter
欧芹 650	ōu qín 650	ou chyn 650	650 parsley
衬衣 781	chèn yī 781	chenn i 781	781 shirt
衬衫 114	chèn shān 114	chenn shan 114	114 blouse
和平 656	hé píng 656	her pyng 656	656 peace
季节 762	jì jié 762	jih jye 762	762 season

Simplified Chinese	Pinyin (with tone-accents)	Romanized transliteration	English
虱子 534	shīzi 534	shytz 534	534 louse
雨 709	yǔ 709	yeu 709	709 rain
雨衣 710	yǔ yī 710	yeu i 710	710 raincoat
金 412	jīn 412	jin 412	412 gold
金发 112	jīn fà 112	jin fa 112	112 blonde
鱼 355	yú 355	yu 355	355 fish
9 画 面包 129	miàn bāo 129	miann bau 129	129 bread
面包师傅 62	miàn bāo shī fù 62	miann bau shy fuh 62	62 baker
面条 613	miàn tiáo 613	miann tyau 613	613 noodle
面粉 361	miàn fěn 361	miann feen 361	361 flour
重 448	zhòng 448	jonq 448	448 heavy
重复 723	chóng fù 723	chorng fuh 723	723 repeat
重量 972	zhòng liàng 972	jonq liang 972	972 weight
说服 664	shuō fú 664	shuo fwu 664	664 persuade
语言 501	yǔ yán 501	yeu yan 501	501 language
南边 818	nánbian 818	nan-bian 818	818 south
厚 876	hòu 876	how 876	876 thick
首都 156	shǒu dū 156	shoou du 156	156 capital
信 517	xìn 517	shinn 517	517 letter
信封 322	xìn fēng 322	shinn feng 322	322 envelope

Simplified Chinese	Pinyin (with tone-accents)	Romanized transliteration	English
便宜 180	piányi 180	pyan-yi 180	180 cheap
便秘 216	biàn bì 216	biann bih 216	216 constipation
便道 788	biàn dào 788	biann daw 788	788 sidewalk
保证 423	bǎo zhèng 423	bao jenq 423	423 guaranty
保险 476	bǎo xiǎn 476	bao shean 476	476 insurance
建筑物 141	jiàn zhù wù 141	jiann juh wuh 141	141 building
降落伞 646	jiàng luò sǎn 646	jianq luoh saan 646	646 parachute
兔子 707	tùzi 707	tuhtz 707	707 rabbit
勇气 230	yǒng qì 230	yeong chih 230	230 courage
洋白菜 150	yáng bái cài 150	yang bair tsay 150	150 cabbage
洋葱 631	yáng cōng 631	yang tsong 631	631 onion
洗 963	xǐ 963	shii 963	963 wash
洗衣店 505	xǐ yī diàn 505	shii i diann 505	505 laundry
洗澡 72	xǐ zǎo 72	shii tzao 72	72 bath
客人 424	kè rén 424	keh ren 424	424 guest
闻 806	wén 806	wen 806	806 smell
送 259	sòng 259	songq 259	259 deliver
送 769	sòng 769	songq 769	769 send
挂 436	guà 436	guah 436	436 hang
挂号 718	guà hào 718	guah haw 718	718 registered

Simplified Chinese	Pinyin (with tone-accents)	Romanized transliteration	English
指甲 353	zhǐ jiǎ 353	jyy jea 353	353 fingernail
项链 598	xiàng liàn 598	shiang liann 598	598 necklace
草 418	cǎo 418	tsao 418	418 grass
草坪 506	cǎo píng 506	tsao pyng 506	506 lawn
药 560	yào 560	yaw 560	560 medicine
药房 665	yào fáng 665	yaw farng 665	665 pharmacy
药品 297	yào pǐn 297	yaw piin 297	297 drug
咳嗽 227	ké sòu 227	ker sow 227	227 cough
哑巴 590	yǎba 590	yea-ba 590	590 mute
哪里？977	nǎli? 977	naa-lii? 977	977 where?
帮助 450	bāng zhù 450	bang juh 450	450 help
带来 136	dài lái 136	day lai 136	136 bring
带路人 425	dài lù rén 425	day luh ren 425	425 guide
律师 507	lǜ shī 507	liuh shy 507	507 lawyer
很 948	hěn 948	heen 948	948 very
狮子 526	shīzi 526	shytz 526	526 lion
独自 24	dú zì 24	dwu tzyh 24	24 alone
屋子 736	wūzi 736	utz 736	736 room
屋顶 735	wū dǐng 735	u diing 735	735 roof
弯路 265	wān lù 265	uan luh 265	265 detour

Simplified Chinese	Pinyin (with tone-accents)	Romanized transliteration	English
娃娃 54	wáwa 54	wa-wa 54	54 baby
结婚 552	jié hūn 552	jye huen 552	552 marriage
给 404	gěi 404	geei 404	404 give
绘画 641	huì huà 641	huey huah 641	641 painting
点 686	diǎn 686	dean 686	686 point
点心 263	diǎn xīn 263	dean shin 263	263 dessert
玻璃 406	bōli 406	bo-li 406	406 glass
标记 789	biāo jì 789	biau jih 789	789 sign
相信 91	xiāng xìn 91	shiang shinn 91	91 believe
柚子 417	yòuzi 417	yowtz 417	417 grapefruit
栎树 622	lì shù 622	lih shuh 622	622 oak
树 919	shù 919	shuh 919	919 tree
咸饼 233	xián bǐng 233	shyan biing 233	233 cracker
战争 961	zhàn zhēng 961	jann jeng 961	961 war
春天 824	chūn tiān 824	chuen tian 824	824 spring
是 75	shì 75	shyh 75	75 be
是 997	shì 997	shyh 997	997 yes
显示 785	xiǎn shì 785	shean shyh 785	785 show
星星 830	xīngxing 830	shing-shing 830	830 star
星期 971	xīng qī 971	shing chi 971	971 week

Simplified Chinese	Pinyin (with tone-accents)	Romanized transliteration	English
星期一 571	xīng qī yī 571	shing chi i 571	571 Monday
星期二 924	xīng qī èr 924	shing chi ell 924	924 Tuesday
星期三 970	xīng qī sān 970	shing chi san 970	970 Wednesday
星期四 891	xīng qī sì 891	shing chi syh 891	891 Thursday
星期五 381	xīng qī wǔ 381	shing chi wuu 381	381 Friday
星期六 751	xīng qī liù 751	shing chi liow 751	751 Saturday
星期天 851	xīng qī tiān 851	shing chi tian 851	851 Sunday
昨天 998	zuó tiān 998	tzwo tian 998	998 yesterday
泉 373	quán 373	chyuan 373	373 fountain
贵 330	guì 330	guey 330	330 expensive
费用 224	fèiyong 224	fey-yong 224	224 cost
费用 329	fèiyòng 329	fey-yonq 329	329 expense
胡子 79	húzi 79	hwutz 79	79 beard
胡萝卜 165	hú luóbo 165	hwu luo-bo 165	165 carrot
胡椒 661	hú jiāo 661	hwu jiau 661	661 pepper
背包 494	bēi bāo 494	beji bau 494	494 knapsack
背叛 98	bèi pàn 98	bey pann 98	98 betray
背脊 56	bèi jǐ 56	bey jii 56	56 back
胆囊 393	dǎn náng 393	daan nang 393	393 gall-bladder
胃 838	wèi 838	wey 838	838 stomach

Simplified Chinese	Pinyin (with tone-accents)	Romanized transliteration	English
肺脏 539	fèi zàng 539	fey tzanq 539	539 lung
毒 687	dú 687	dwu 687	687 poison
疯狂 236	fēng kuáng 236	feng kwang 236	236 crazy
砖 133	zhuān 133	juan 133	133 brick
看见 766	kàn jiàn 766	kann jiann 766	766 see
钢 834	gāng 834	gang 834	834 steel
钢笔 659	gāng bǐ 659	gang bii 659	659 pen
钥匙 490	yàoshi 490	yaw-shy 490	490 key
科学 756	kē xué 756	ke shyue 756	756 science
秋天 51	qiū tiān 51	chiou tian 51	51 autumn
香料 821	xiāng liào 821	shiang liaw 821	821 spice
香肠 752	xiāng cháng 752	shiang charng 752	752 sausage
美丽 80	měi lì 80	meei lih 80	80 beautiful
籽 767	zǐ 767	tzyy 767	767 seed
蚂蚁 34	mǎ yǐ 34	maa yii 34	34 ant
食物 365	shí wù 365	shyr wuh 365	365 food
食堂 271	shí táng 271	shyr tarng 271	271 dining room
食欲 37	shí yù 37	shyr yuh 37	37 appetite
夏天 849 (10画)	xià tiān 849	shiah tian 849	849 summer
高 863	gāo 863	gau 863	863 tall

Simplified Chinese	Pinyin (with tone-accents)	Romanized transliteration	English
高兴 405	gāo xìng 405	gau shinq 405	405 glad
高度 27	gāo dù 27	gau duh 27	27 altitude
请 681	qǐng 681	chiing 681	681 please
读 714	dú 714	dwu 714	714 read
谁? 979	shuí? 979	shwei? 979	979 who?
真 401	zhēn 401	jen 401	401 genuine
真实 922	zhēn shí 922	jen shyr 922	922 truth
拿 862	ná 862	na 862	862 take
借款 254	jiè kuǎn 254	jieh koan 254	254 debt
倾复 157	qīng fù 157	ching fuh 157	157 capsize
能 1	néng 1	neng 1	1 able
难看 931	nán kàn 931	nan kann 931	931 ugly
院子 396	yuànzi 396	yuanntz 396	396 garden
陪伴 6	péi bàn 6	peir bann 6	6 accompany
陪嫁钱, 288	péi jià qián 288	peir jiah chyan 288	288 dowry
部分 651	bùfen 651	buh-fen 651	651 part
消化 270	xiāo huà 270	shiau huah 270	270 digestion
消夫 275	xiāo shī 275	shiau shy 275	275 disappear
消息 473	xiāo xī 473	shiau shi 473	473 information
浴衣 73	yù yī 73	yuh i 73	73 bathrobe

Simplified Chinese	Pinyin (with tone-accents)	Romanized transliteration	English
海 760	hǎi 760	hae 760	760 sea
海关 245	hǎi guān 245	hae guan 245	245 customs
海岛 482	hǎi dǎo 482	hae dao 482	482 island
海绵 822	hǎi mián 822	hae mian 822	822 sponge
海滩 76	hǎi tān 76	hae tan 76	76 beach
害怕 343	hài pà 343	hay pah 343	343 fear
家具 391	jiā jù 391	jia jiuh 391	391 furniture
家畜 170	jiā chù 170	jia chuh 170	170 cattle
家族 337	jiā zú 337	jia tzwu 337	337 family
容易 309	róng yì 309	rong yih 309	309 easy
透明 917	tòu míng 917	tow ming 917	917 transparent
透镜 516	tòu jìng 516	tow jinq 516	516 lens
捕获 158	bǔ huò 158	buu huoh 158	158 capture
损失 533	sǔn shī 533	soen shy 533	533 loss
损害 247	sǔn hài 247	soen hay 247	247 damage
菜花 171	cài huā 171	tsay hua 171	171 cauliflower
菜单 563	cài dān 563	tsay dan 563	563 menu
荷兰石竹 163	hé lán shí zhú 163	her lan shyr jwu 163	163 carnation
获得 392	huò dé 392	huoh der 392	392 gain
哭 241	kū 241	ku 241	241 cry

Simplified Chinese	Pinyin (with tone-accents)	Romanized transliteration	English
唤醒 53	huàn xǐng 53	huann shiing 53	53 awaken
圆 193	yuán 193	yuan 193	193 circle
圆 739	yuán 739	yuan 739	739 round
饿 466	è 466	eh 466	466 hungry
展览会 326	zhǎn lǎn huì 326	jaan laan huey 326	326 exhibition (display)
旅行 918	lǚ xíng 918	leu shyng 918	918 travel
烤 734	kǎo 734	kao 734	734 roast
烘 61	hōng 61	hong 61	61 bake
烟 807	yān 807	ian 807	807 smoke
烟筒 188	yāntong 188	ian-toong 188	188 chimney
热 460	rè 460	reh 460	460 hot
恶意 546	è yì 546	eh yih 546	546 malicious
样品 749	yàng pǐn 749	yanq piin 749	749 sample
桔子 635	júzi 635	jyutz 635	635 orange
桌子 859	zhuōzi 859	juotz 859	859 table
桥 135	qiáo 135	chyau 135	135 bridge
根 737	gēn 737	gen 737	737 root
晕船 761	yùn chuán 761	yunn chwan 761	761 seasick
浆果 96	jiāng guǒ 96	jiang guoo 96	96 berry
拳头 356	quántou 356	chyuan-tou 356	356 fist

Simplified Chinese	Pinyin (with tone-accents)	Romanized transliteration	English
敌人 320	dí rén 320	dyi ren 320	320 enemy
爱 535	ài 535	ay 535	535 love
胶 408	jiāo 408	jiau 408	408 glue
脑子 126	nǎozi 126	naotz 126	126 brain
脏 274	zāng 274	tzang 274	274 dirty
胳臂 42	gēbei 42	ge-bey 42	42 arm
脆 377	cuì 377	tsuey 377	377 fragile
胸脯 131	xiōng pú 131	shiong pwu 131	131 breast
胸膛 185	xiōng táng 185	shiong tarng 185	185 chest
脂肪 341	zhī fáng 341	jy farng 341	341 fat
窄 595	zhǎi 595	jae 595	595 narrow
站 829	zhàn 829	jann 829	829 stand
站台 677	zhàn tái 677	jann tair 677	677 platform
竞赛 213	jìng sài 213	jinq say 213	213 competition
病 472	bìng 472	binq 472	472 illness
被害者 949	bèi hài zhě 949	bey hay jee 949	949 victim
被禁止 367	bèi jìn zhǐ 367	bey jin jyy 367	367 forbidden
破布 708	pò bù 708	poh buh 708	708 rag
破坏 264	pò huài 264	poh huay 264	264 destroy
留 720	liú 720	liou 720	720 remain

Simplified Chinese	Pinyin (with tone-accents)	Romanized transliteration	English
盐 748	yán 748	yan 748	748 salt
监狱 699	jiān yù 699	jian yuh 699	699 prison
钱包 702	qián bāo 702	chyan bau 702	702 purse
钳子 683	qiánzi 683	chyantz 683	683 plier(s)
铃子 92	língzi 92	lingtz 92	92 bell
铁 480	tiě 480	tiee 480	480 iron
铅 509	qiān 509	chian 509	509 lead
铅笔 660	qiān bǐ 660	chian bii 660	660 pencil
秘密 764	mì mì 764	mih mih 764	764 secret
鸭子 300	yāzi 300	iatz 300	300 duck
粉末 696	fěn mò 696	feen moh 696	696 powder
粉红色 674	fěn hóng sè 674	feen horng seh 674	674 pink
顽固 847	wán gù 847	wan guh 847	847 stubborn
蚊子 577	wénzi 577	wentz 577	577 mosquito
笑 504	xiào 504	shiaw 504	504 laugh
笑话 487	xiàohuà 487	shiaw-huah 487	487 joke
缺席 3	quē xí 3	chiue shyi 3	3 absent
臭虫 83	chòu chóng 83	chow chorng 83	83 bedbug
素描 289	sù miáo 289	suh miau 289	289 drawing
紧急 941	jǐn jí 941	jiin jyi 941	941 urgent

Simplified Chinese	Pinyin (with tone-accents)	Romanized transliteration	English
起立 731	qǐ lì 731	chii lih 731	rise
起重机 234	qǐ zhòng jī 234	chii jonq ji 234	crane
11画 骨头 119	gútou 119	gwu-tou 119	bone
商人 564	shāng rén 564	shang ren 564	merchant
商店 841	shāng diàn 841	shang diann 841	store
离开 513	lí kāi 513	li kai 513	leave (to depart)
离婚 280	lí hūn 280	li huen 280	divorce
减少 717	jiǎn shǎo 717	jean shao 717	reduce
谎话 518	huǎng huà 518	hoang huah 518	lie
黄 996	huáng 996	hwang 996	yellow
黄瓜 242	huáng guā 242	hwang gua 242	cucumber
黄油 146	huáng yóu 146	hwang you 146	butter
黄铜 128	huáng tóng 128	hwang torng 128	brass
停止 840	tíng zhǐ 840	tyng jyy 840	stop
停车 649	tíng chē 649	tyng che 649	parking
做 544	zuò 544	tzuoh 544	make
健康 445	jiàn kāng 445	jiann kang 445	health
偷 833	tōu 833	tou 833	steal
假期 943	jià qī 943	jiah chi 943	vacation
剪子 757	jiǎnzi 757	jeantz 757	scissors

Simplified Chinese	Pinyin (with tone-accents)	Romanized transliteration	English
液体 528	yè tǐ 528	yeh tii 528	528 liquid
深 256	shēn 256	shen 256	256 deep
清楚 196	qīng chǔ 196	ching chuu 196	196 clear
淋浴 786	lín yù 786	lin yuh 786	786 shower
淹 296	yān 296	ian 296	296 drown
惊讶 853	jīng yà 853	jing yah 853	853 surprise
蜜蜂 84	mì fēng 84	mih feng 84	84 bee
麻烦 920	máfan 920	ma-farn 920	920 trouble
接吻 492	jiē wěn 492	jie woen 492	492 kiss
接受 4	jiē shòu 4	jie show 4	4 accept
掉 295	diào 295	diaw 295	295 drop
堂兄弟 231	táng xiōng dì 231	tarng shiong dih 231	231 cousin
唱 793	chàng 793	chanq 793	793 sing
啤酒 86	pí jiǔ 86	pyi jeou 86	86 beer
梦 290	mèng 290	menq 290	290 dream
猪 669	zhū 669	ju 669	669 pig
猪肉 689	zhū ròu 689	ju row 689	689 pork
猫 168	māo 168	mhau 168	168 cat
婚礼 969	hūn lǐ 969	huen lii 969	969 wedding
绳子 738	shéngzi 738	sherngtz 738	738 rope

Simplified Chinese	Pinyin (with tone-accents)	Romanized transliteration	English
绷带 65	bēng dài 65	beng day 65	65 bandage
绿色 420	lǜ sè 420	liuh seh 420	420 green
烧 118	shāo 118	shau 118	118 boil
烧 143	shāo 143	shau 143	143 burn
球 64	qiú 64	chyou 64	64 ball
理发师 430	lǐ fà shī 430	lii fa shy 430	430 hairdresser
梳子 209	shūzi 209	shutz 209	209 comb
梯子 498	tīzi 498	titz 498	498 ladder
梨子 657	lízi 657	litz 657	657 pear
桶 68	tǒng 68	toong 68	68 barrel
瓶子 122	píngzi 122	pyngtz 122	122 bottle
匙子 823	chízi 823	chyrtz 823	823 spoon
教堂 191	jiào táng 191	jiaw tarng 191	191 church
救援 724	jiù yuán 724	jiow yuan 724	724 rescue
脖子 597	bózi 597	bortz 597	597 neck
脚 366	jiǎo 366	jeau 366	366 foot
脚尖 902	jiǎo jiān 902	jeau jian 902	902 toe
脚后跟 449	jiǎo hòu gēn 449	jeau how gen 449	449 heel
脚脖子 32	jiǎo bózi 32	jeau bortz 32	32 ankle
脸 335	liǎn 335	lean 335	335 face

Simplified Chinese	Pinyin (with tone-accents)	Romanized transliteration	English
聋子 252	lóngzi 252	longtz 252	252 deaf
眺望 950	tiào wàng 950	tiaw wang 950	950 view
眼泪 868	yǎn lèi 868	yean ley 868	868 tears
眼睛 333	yǎn jīng 333	yean jing 333	333 eye
眼镜 334	yǎn jìng 334	yean jinq 334	334 eyeglasses
累 900	lèi 900	ley 900	900 tired
盘子 276	pánzi 276	parntz 276	276 dish
铜 219	tóng 219	torng 219	219 copper
银 792	yín 792	yn 792	792 silver
职业 700	zhí yè 700	jyr yeh 700	700 profession
票 892	piào 892	piaw 892	892 ticket
领带 894	lǐng dài 894	liing day 894	894 tie
蛇 808	shé 808	sher 808	808 snake
甜 856	tián 856	tyan 856	856 sweet
船 116	chuán 116	chwan 116	116 boat
野营 154	yě yíng 154	yee yng 154	154 camp
距离 277	jù lí 277	jiuh li 277	277 distance
雪 809	xuě 809	sheue 809	809 snow
雪橇 802	xuě qiāo 802	sheue chiau 802	802 sled
12画 谢谢 873	xièxie 873	shieh-shieh 873	873 thanks

Simplified Chinese	Pinyin (with tone-accents)	Romanized transliteration	English
厨房 493	chú fáng 493	chwu farng 493	493 kitchen
傍晚 323	bàng wǎn 323	banq woan 323	323 evening
渡船 346	dù chuán 346	duh chwan 346	346 ferry
游泳 857	yóu yǒng 857	you yeong 857	857 swim
港口 437	gǎng kǒu 437	gaang koou 437	437 harbor
湖 499	hú 499	hwu 499	499 lake
湿 975	shī 975	shy 975	975 wet
渴 881	kě 881	kee 881	881 thirst
愉快 680	yú kuài 680	yu kuay 680	680 pleasant
寒冷 206	hán lěng 206	harn leeng 206	206 cold
富裕 726	fù yù 726	fuh yuh 726	726 rich
廉价品 66	lián jià pǐn 66	lian jiah piin 66	66 bargain
道路 967	dào lù 967	daw luh 967	967 way
遇见 561	yù jiàn 561	yuh jiann 561	561 meet
葬礼 389	zàng lǐ 389	tzanq lii 389	389 funeral
葡萄 416	pútao 416	pwu-taur 416	416 grape
葡萄酒 984	pú táo jiǔ 984	pwu taur jeou 984	984 wine
喝 292	hē 292	he 292	292 drink
喉咙 887	hóu lóng 887	hour long 887	887 throat
帽子 440	màozi 440	mawtz 440	440 hat

Simplified Chinese	Pinyin (with tone-accents)	Romanized transliteration	English
街道 845	jiē dào 845	jie daw 845	845 street
强 846	qiáng 846	chyang 846	846 strong
悲哀 744	bēi āi 744	bei ai 744	744 sad
悲痛 815	bēi tòng 815	bei tonq 815	815 sorrow
棋 184	qí 184	chyi 184	184 chess
植物 676	zhí wù 676	jyr wuh 676	676 plant
森林 369	sēn lín 369	sen lin 369	369 forest
椅子 177	yǐzi 177	yiitz 177	177 chair
棍子 835	gùnzi 835	guenntz 835	835 stick
棉布 225	mián bù 225	mian buh 225	225 cotton
裁缝店 861	cáifeng diàn 861	tzair-fenq diann 861	861 tailor
晚 503	wǎn 503	woan 503	503 late
晚上 607	wǎnshang 607	woan-shanq 607	607 night
晚餐 272	wǎn cān 272	woan tsan 272	272 dinner
犊子 152	dúzi 152	dwutz 152	152 calf
犊肉 945	dú ròu 945	dwu row 945	945 veal
期待 328	qī dài 328	chi day 328	328 expect
窗户 983	chuānghu 983	chuang-huh 983	983 window
窗帘 244	chuāng lián 244	chuang lian 244	244 curtain
痛苦 640	tòng kǔ 640	tonq kuu 640	640 pain

Simplified Chinese	Pinyin (with tone-accents)	Romanized transliteration	English
裤子 921	kùzi 921	kuhtz 921	921 trousers
裙子 800	qúnzi 800	chyuntz 800	800 skirt
硬 438	yìng 438	yinq 438	438 hard
锁 531	suǒ 531	suoo 531	531 lock
锅 694	guō 694	guo 694	694 pot
短 783	duǎn 783	doan 783	783 short
税 866	shuì 866	shuey 866	866 tax
程度 258	chéng dù 258	cherng duh 258	258 degree
鸽子 670	gēzi 670	getz 670	670 pigeon
鹅 415	é 415	er 415	415 goose
疏忽 601	shūhu 601	shu-hu 601	601 negligent
蛙子 384	wāzi 384	uatz 384	384 frog
等 957	děng 957	deeng 957	957 wait
登 198	dēng 198	deng 198	198 climb
跑 741	pǎo 741	pao 741	741 run
跑道 742	pǎo dào 742	pao daw 742	742 runway
跛子 240	bǒzi 240	bootz 240	240 cripple
黑 106	hēi 106	hei 106	106 black
黑暗 249	hēi àn 249	hei ann 249	249 dark
13画 谨慎 172	jǐn shèn 172	jiin shenn 172	172 caution

Simplified Chinese	Pinyin (with tone-accents)	Romanized transliteration	English
满期 331	mǎn qī 331	maan chi 331	331 expire
搬 166	bān 166	ban 166	166 carry
搬 915	bān 915	ban 915	915 transfer
搬运人 691	bān yùn rén 691	ban yunn ren 691	691 porter
蓝 115	lán 115	lan 115	115 blue
嫉妒 485	jídu 485	jyi-duh 485	485 jealous
缝纫 775	féng rèn 775	ferng renn 775	775 sewing
煎饼 644	jiānbing 644	jian-biing 644	644 pancake
煤 202	méi 202	mei 202	202 coal
想 880	xiǎng 880	sheang 880	880 think
想起 721	xiǎngqi 721	sheang-chii 721	721 remember
楼上 940	lóu shàng 940	lou shang 940	940 upstairs
楼梯 826	lóu tī 826	lou ti 826	826 staircase
暖炉 843	nuǎn lú 843	noan lu 843	843 stove
暖和 962	nuǎnhuo 962	noan-huo 962	962 warm
数字 619	shù zì 619	shuh tzyh 619	619 number
新 605	xīn 605	shin 605	605 new
新娘 134	xīn niáng 134	shin niang 134	134 bride
新鲜 380	xīn xiān 380	shin shian 380	380 fresh
腰带 95	yāo dài 95	iau day 95	95 belt

Simplified Chinese	Pinyin (with tone-accents)	Romanized transliteration	English
腮 181	sāi 181	sai 181	181 cheek
腿 515	tuǐ 515	toei 515	515 leg
碗 123	wǎn 123	woan 123	123 bowl
睡觉 803	shuì jiào 803	shuey jiaw 803	803 sleep
错误 570	cuò wù 570	tsuoh wuh 570	570 mistake
错误 994	cuò wù 994	tsuoh wuh 994	994 wrong
锡 897	xī 897	shi 897	897 tin
锤子 433	chuízi 433	chweitz 433	433 hammer
锯子 753	jùzi 753	jiuhtz 753	753 saw
蜂蜜 456	fēng mì 456	feng mih 456	456 honey
辞典 268	cí diǎn 268	tsyr dean 268	268 dictionary
签名 790	qiān míng 790	chian ming 790	790 signature
跳入 278	tiào rù 278	tiaw ruh 278	278 dive
跳蚤 359	tiào zǎo 359	tiaw tzao 359	359 flea
解冻 874	jiě dòng 874	jiee donq 874	874 thaw
雷声 890	léi shēng 890	lei sheng 890	890 thunder
零 1000	líng 1000	ling 1000	1000 zero
罗 364	wù 364	wuh 364	364 fog
鼓 298	gǔ 298	guu 298	298 drum
14[周] 漂白 110	piǎo bái 110	peau bair 110	110 bleach

Simplified Chinese	Pinyin (with tone-accents)	Romanized transliteration	English
慢慢 804	màn màn 804	mann mhan 804	804 slowly
赛马 458	sài mǎ 458	say maa 458	458 horserace
寡妇 981	guǎfu 981	goa-fuh 981	981 widow
墙 960	qiáng 960	chyang 960	960 wall
熊 78	xióng 78	shyong 78	78 bear
膀胱 107	páng guāng 107	parng guang 107	107 bladder
歌 814	gē 814	ge 814	814 song
褐色 139	hè sè 139	heh seh 139	139 brown
链子 176	liànzi 176	lianntz 176	176 chain
蜡烛 155	là zhú 155	lah jwu 155	155 candle
算 228	suàn 228	suann 228	228 count
算账 7	suàn zhàng 7	suann janq 7	7 account
鼻子 616	bízi 616	byitz 616	616 nose
酸 817	suān 817	suan 817	817 sour
15画 谴责 108	qiǎn zé 108	chean tzer 108	108 blame
潮 893	cháo 893	chaur 893	893 tide
憎恨 441	zēng hèn 441	tzeng henn 441	441 hate
墨水 474	mò shuǐ 474	moh shoei 474	474 ink
疏菜 946	shū cài 946	shu tsay 946	946 vegetable
熨 481	yùn 481	yunn 481	481 ironing

Simplified Chinese	Pinyin (with tone-accents)	Romanized transliteration	English
横过 8	héng guò 8	herng guoh 8	8 across
樱桃 183	yīng táo 183	ing taur 183	183 cherry
橡胶 740	xiàng jiāo 740	shiang jiau 740	740 rubber
暴风雨 842	bào fēng yǔ 842	baw feng yeu 842	842 storm
膝 495	xī 495	shi 495	495 knee
褥垫 554	rù diàn 554	ruh diann 554	554 mattress
瞎 111	xiā 111	shia 111	111 blind
镇 911	zhèn 911	jenn 911	911 town
颜色 208	yán sè 208	yan seh 208	208 color
蝴蝶 147	hú dié 147	hwu dye 147	147 butterfly
豌豆 655	wān dòu 655	uan dow 655	655 pea
醋 952	cù 952	tsuh 952	952 vinegar
鲨鱼 776	shā yú 776	sha yu 776	776 shark
鞍 745	ān 745	an 745	745 saddle
鞋 782	xié 782	shye 782	782 shoe
16画 澡盆 74	zǎo pén 74	tzao pern 74	74 bathtub
懒惰 508	lǎn duò 508	laan duoh 508	508 lazy
薄 879	báo 879	baur 879	879 thin
嘴 581	zuǐ 581	tzoei 581	581 mouth
嘴唇 527	zuǐ chún 527	tzoei chwen 527	527 lip

Simplified Chinese	Pinyin (with tone-accents)	Romanized transliteration	English
噪音 612	zào yīn 612	tzaw in 612	612 noise
燕麦 624	yàn mài 624	yann may 624	624 oats
橹 623	lǔ 623	luu 623	623 oar
镜子 568	jìngzi 568	jinqtz 568	568 mirror
糕 151	gāo 151	gau 151	151 cake
糕点 652	gāo diǎn 652	gau dean 652	652 pastry
糖 848	táng 848	tarng 848	848 sugar
篮子 71	lánzi 71	lantz 71	71 basket
辩解 325	biàn jiě 325	biann jiee 325	325 excuse
鲱鱼 452	fēi yú 452	fei yu 452	452 herring
17画 蟑螂 204	zhānglang 204	jang-lang 204	204 cockroach
螺丝 759	luó sī 759	luo sy 759	759 screw
18画 糨糊 831	jiànghu 831	jiang-hwu 831	831 starch
翻译 478	fān yì 478	fan yih 478	478 interpreter
翻译 916	fān yì 916	fan yih 916	916 translate
19画 蘑菇 588	mógu 588	mo-gu 588	588 mushroom
鳕鱼 205	xuě yú 205	sheue yu 205	205 codfish
20画 雹 428	xiàn 428	shiann 428	428 hail
21画 魔术 541	mó shù 541	mo shuh 541	541 magic
23画 鼹鼠 580	xǐ shǔ 580	shi shuu 580	580 mouse

The Pinyin Transliteration

(alphabetized, according to pronunciation)

The Chinese language does not use an alphabet. Each word in Chinese is portrayed by a graphic sign representing the object or idea. Often two or more such signs are combined to express different word meanings. On the following pages all of the Chinese words in this Basic Dictionary are arranged in alphabetical order based on the new official Phonetic system, called *Pinyin*. Literally, "pīn" means to assemble, and "yīn" the sound of the vowel.

The Four Tone Accents

The new phonetic arrangement of the official (Mandarin) language differentiates four levels of intonation. The tone signifies raising or lowering the voice when a syllable is pronounced. The tone sign which is like an accent above the vowel covers the whole syllable or word.

Some syllables are "tone-less" and therefore not accented.

Tone	Sign	Short description
1.	-	Constant high pitch
2.	´	Start low, raise slightly to high pitch
3.	ˇ	Voice is dropped, and then raises again
4.	`	Start at high pitch, then down sharply

A short explanation of the Phonetic Alphabet

According to the recent decision of China's State Council the new phonetic alphabet with the *approximate* English equivalents is pronounced as follows (the traditional system of Romanization is given in brackets):

a (a), as in "far"

b (p), as in "be"

c (ts), as t plus s in "its"; but

ch (ch), as t plus sh in "chat," aspirated

d (t), as in "do"

e (e), as in "her" (or the German umlauted ö); but

ei, as in "way" (a diphthong)

f (f), as in "foot"

g (k), as in "go"

h (h), as in "her," aspirated

i (i), has two sounds:
   1) as in "eat," and
   2) as in "sir" in syllables beginning with the con-
    sonants c, ch, r, s, sh, z and zh

ie, a diphthong, as in "yes"

j (ch), as in "jeep"

k (k), as in "kind," aspirated

l (l), as in "land"

m (m), as in "me"

n (n), as in "no"

o (o), as in "law"

p (p), as in "part," strongly aspirated

q (ch), as ch in "cheek"

r (j), retroflex, not rolled, or like z in "azure"

s (s, ss, sz), as in "sister"; and

sh (sh), as in "shore"

t (t), as in "top," strongly aspirated

u (u), as in "too," also as in the French u in "tu" or the
   German umlauted ü in "München"

v (v), only for foreign words

w (w), a semi-vowel in syllables beginning with u when
   not preceded by a consonant, pronounced as in
   "want" (with both lips)

x (hs), as sh in "she"

y, a semi-vowel in syllables beginning with i or u when
   not preceded by a consonant, pronounced as in "yet"

z (ts, tz), as in "zero"; and

zh (ch), as j in "jump"

The Pinyin Transliteration

(alphabetized, according to pronunciation)

ài 535	love
ān 745	saddle
ān jìng 706	quiet
ān quán 746	safety
ān quán dài 520	life belt
ān wèi 211	comfort
bā 313	eight
bā shí 315	eighty
bá yuè 48	August
bái 978	white
bǔi 465	hundred
bān 166	carry
bān 915	transfer
bān yùn rén 691	porter
bàn jiù 763	second-hand
bàn shì chù 627	office
bāng zhù 450	help
bàng wǎn 323	evening
bāo 59	bag
bāo guǒ 647	parcel

bào 879	thin
bǎo shí 486	jewel
bǎo xiǎn 476	insurance
bǎo zhèng 423	guaranty
bào fēng yǔ 842	storm
bào zhǐ 606	newspaper
bèi āi 744	sad
bèi bāo 494	knapsack
bèi tòng 815	sorrow
bēizi 243	cup
bèi biān 615	north
bèi hài zhě 949	victim
bèi jǐ 56	back
bèi jìn zhǐ 367	forbidden
bèi pàn 98	betray
bēng dài 65	bandage
bǐ sài 394	game
bízi 616	nose
bì yào 599	need
biān jiè 121	border

The Pinyin Transliteration

(alphabetized, according to pronunciation)

biàn bì 216	constipation	
biàn dào 788	sidewalk	
biàn huà 179	change	
biàn jiě 325	excuse	
biāo jì 789	sign	
biǎo 965	watch	
biǎo miàn 852	surface	
bié zhēn 672	pin	
bīng 469	ice	
bīng qí lín 470	ice cream	
bìng 472	illness	
bōli 406	glass	
bó fù 933	uncle	
bózi 597	neck	
bózi 240	cripple	
bǔ huò 158	capture	
bù 611	no	
bù qiāng 727	rifle	
bù tóng 269	different	
bùfen 651	part	
cāi chǎn 701	property	
cáifeng diàn 861	tailor	
cài dān 563	menu	
cài huā 171	cauliflower	
cāng bái 643	pale	
cāng yíng 363	fly	
cǎo 418	grass	
cǎo píng 506	lawn	
cè suǒ 904	toilet (WC)	
chāzi 371	fork	
cháng 532	long	
cháng shā fā yǐ 226	couch	
cháng wàzi 837	stockings	
chàng 793	sing	
cháo 893	tide	
chǎo jī dàn 758	scrambled eggs	
chē 159	car	
chē fèi 339	fare	
chē lún 976	wheel	
chē zhàn 832	station	

The Pinyin Transliteration

(alphabetized, according to pronunciation)

chèn shān 114	blouse	
chèn yī 781	shirt	
chéng dù 258	degree	
chéng shú 730	ripe	
chéng zhǎng 422	growing	
chī 310	eat	
chízi 823	spoon	
chì luǒ luǒ 593	naked	
chōng mǎn 388	full	
chóng fù 723	repeat	
chòu chóng 83	bedbug	
chū fā 261	departure	
chū hàn 663	perspire	
chū kǒu 327	exit	
chū xiàn 36	appear	
chú fáng 493	kitchen	
chuán 116	boat	
chuán rǎn xìng 217	contagious	
chuāng lián 244	curtain	
chuānghu 983	window	

chuáng 82	bed	
chuáng dān 780	sheets	
chuī shì yuán 218	cook	
chuízi 433	hammer	
chūn tiān 824	spring	
cí 990	word	
cí diǎn 268	dictionary	
cì 836	sting	
cóng 385	from	
cù 952	vinegar	
cuì 377	fragile	
cūn 951	village	
cún jú hòu lǐngdì yóu jiàn 400	general delivery	
cuò wù 570	mistake	
cuò wù 994	wrong	
dǎ dǔ 97	bet	
dǎ fān 939	upset	
dǎ liè 467	hunt	
dǎ zì jī 930	typewriter	
dà 502	large	

The Pinyin Transliteration

(alphabetized, according to pronunciation)

dà lǐ shí 549 marble
dà mài 67 barley
dà suàn 397 garlic
dà tuǐ 878 thigh
dài lái 136 bring
dài lù rén 425 guide
dān shēn hàn 55 bachelor
dǎn náng 393 gall-bladder
dàn shēng 103 birth
dǎo guǎn 675 pipe (tube)
dào 938 until
dào dá 43 arrival
dào lù 967 way
dēng 198 climb
děng 957 wait
dí rén 320 enemy
dì bǎn 360 floor
dì qiú 306 earth
dì tǎn 164 carpet
dì tú 548 map

dì xià shì 69 basement
dì xià shì 173 cellar
dì xià tiě dào 935 underground (subway)
dì xiōng 138 brother
dì zhèn 307 earthquake
dì zhǐ 9 address
diǎn 686 point
diǎn xīn 263 dessert
diàn dēng pào 522 light bulb
diàn tī 317 elevator (lift)
diàn yǐng 583 movie
diào 295 drop
diào kù dài 854 suspenders
diào wà dài 398 garter
dīng xiāng huā 524 lilac
dīngzi 592 nail
dōng biān 308 east
dōng tiān 985 winter
dòng 582 move
dòng wù 31 animal

The Pinyin Transliteration
(alphabetized, according to pronunciation)

dòuzi 77	77 bean	èr yuè 344	344 February
dú 687	687 poison	fā míng 479	479 invention
dú 714	714 read	fā xiàn 351	351 find
dú ròu 945	945 veal	fān yì 478	478 interpreter
dú zì 24	24 alone	fān yì 916	916 translate
dúzi 152	152 calf	fàn 558	558 meal
dù chuán 346	346 ferry	fàn zuì 239	239 crime
dùzi 93	93 belly	fāng xiàng 273	273 direction
duǎn 783	783 short	fáng zū 722	722 rent
duì 15	15 against	fángzi 462	462 house
duì 642	642 pair	fǎng wèn 954	954 visit
duō shǎo qián? 464	464 how much?	fàng sōng 719	719 relax
é 415	415 goose	fēi jī 20	20 airplane
è 466	466 hungry	fēi yú 452	452 herring
è yì 546	546 malicious	féi zào 810	810 soap
érzi 813	813 son	fèi zàng 539	539 lung
ěr huán 305	305 earring	fèiyong 224	224 cost
ěrduo 303	303 ear	fèi yòng 329	329 expense
èr 929	929 two	fēn gé jiān 212	212 compartment
èr shí 928	928 twenty	fén dì 174	174 cemetery

The Pinyin Transliteration

(alphabetized, according to pronunciation)

fěn hóng sè 674 — 674 pink
fěn mò 696 — 696 powder
fēng 982 — 982 wind
fēng kuáng 236 — 236 crazy
fēng mì 456 — 456 honey
féng rèn 775 — 775 sewing
fū rén 585 — 585 Mrs (addressing)
fú wù yuán 958 — 958 waiter
fù mǔ 648 — 648 parents
fù nǚ 987 — 987 woman
fù qīn 342 — 342 father
fù yù 726 — 726 rich
gān jìng 195 — 195 clean
gān lào 182 — 182 cheese
gān zàng 529 — 529 liver
gān zào 299 — 299 dry
gāng 834 — 834 steel
gāng bǐ 659 — 659 pen
gǎng kǒu 437 — 437 harbor
gāo 151 — 151 cake

gāo 863 — 863 tall
gāo diǎn 652 — 652 pastry
gāo dù 27 — 27 altitude
gāo xìng 405 — 405 glad
gē 814 — 814 song
gēbei 42 — 42 arm
gēzi 670 — 670 pigeon
gěi 404 — 404 give
gēn 737 — 737 root
gèng duō 575 — 575 more
gōng chǎng 336 — 336 factory
gōng jù 907 — 907 tool
gōng lù 453 — 453 highway
gōng niú 638 — 638 ox
gōng yù 35 — 35 apartment
gōng zī 956 — 956 wages
gōng zuò 991 — 991 work
gǒu 282 — 282 dog
gū mǔ 49 — 49 aunt
gútou 119 — 119 bone

The Pinyin Transliteration

(alphabetized, according to pronunciation)

gǔ 298 drum
guā liǎn 777 shave
guā liǎn dāo 713 razor
guāfu 981 widow
guà 436 hang
guà hào 718 registered
guān 199 close
guānxi 215 connection
guāng 521 light
guì 330 expensive
gùnzi 835 stick
guō 694 pot
guó jiā 229 country
guó wài 2 abroad
guǒ jiàng 483 jam (marmalade)
hǎi 760 sea
hǎi dǎo 482 island
hǎi guān 245 customs
hǎi mián 822 sponge
hǎi tān 76 beach

hài pà 343 fear
hán lěng 206 cold
hǎo 23 all right
hǎo 413 good
hē 292 drink
hé 29 and
hé 733 river
hé lán shí zhú 163 carnation
hé píng 656 peace
hè sè 139 brown
hēi 106 black
hēi àn 249 dark
hěn 948 very
héng guò 8 across
hōng 61 bake
hóng 716 red
hóu lóng 887 throat
hòu 876 thick
hú 499 lake
hú dié 147 butterfly

The Pinyin Transliteration

(alphabetized, according to pronunciation)

hú jiāo 661	661 pepper		huǎng huà 518	518 lie
hú luóbo 165	165 carrot		huī chén 301	301 dust
húli 376	376 fox		huī sè 421	421 grey
húzi 79	79 beard		huí 725	725 return
hù xiāng 591	591 mutual		huí dá 33	33 answer
hùshi 620	620 nurse		huì huà 641	641 painting
huā 362	362 flower		huì yuán 562	562 member
huā biān 497	497 lace		hūn lǐ 969	969 wedding
huà 667	667 picture		huǒ 354	354 fire
huà fēn 279	279 divide		huǒ chái 553	553 match
huà kuàng 378	378 frame		huǒ chē 914	914 train
huái yí 286	286 doubt		huǒ jī 925	925 turkey
huài 58	58 bad		huǒ tuǐ 432	432 ham
huān lè 565	565 merry		huò bì 572	572 money
huān yíng 973	973 welcome		huò dé 392	392 gain
huàn xǐng 53	53 awaken		huò wù 162	162 cargo
huáng 996	996 yellow		huò zhě 634	634 or
huáng guā 242	242 cucumber		jī 186	186 chicken
huáng tóng 128	128 brass		jī chǎng 21	21 airport
huáng yóu 146	146 butter		jī dàn 312	312 egg

The Pinyin Transliteration

(alphabetized, according to pronunciation)

jī huì 178	chance	
jī ròu 587	muscle	
jí duān 332	extreme	
jídù 485	jealous	
jì jié 762	season	
jiā chù 170	cattle	
jiā jù 391	furniture	
jiā zú 337	family	
jià qī 943	vacation	
jià zhí 944	value	
jiàqian 697	price	
jiān bǎng 784	shoulder	
jiān guǒ 621	nut	
jiān yù 699	prison	
jiānbing 644	pancake	
jiǎn shǎo 717	reduce	
jiǎnzi 757	scissors	
jiàn kāng 445	health	
jiàn zhù wù 141	building	
jiāng guǒ 96	berry	
jiǎng 820	speak	
jiàng luò sǎn 646	parachute	
jiànghu 831	starch	
jiāo 408	glue	
jiāo qián 654	pay	
jiāo yì suǒ 324	exchange	
jiǎo 366	foot	
jiǎo bózi 32	ankle	
jiǎo hòu gēn 449	heel	
jiǎo jiān 902	toe	
jiào 153	call	
jiào táng 191	church	
jiē dào 845	street	
jiē shòu 4	accept	
jiē wěn 492	kiss	
jié hūn 552	marriage	
jié rì 455	holiday	
jiě dòng 874	thaw	
jiě mèi 794	sister	
jiè huáng 589	mustard	

The Pinyin Transliteration

(alphabetized, according to pronunciation)

jiè kuǎn 254	254 debt	jué bù 604	604 never
jièzhi 729	729 ring	kāi 293	293 drive
jīn 412	412 gold	kāi guān 858	858 switch
jīn fà 112	112 blonde	kāi sāi zuān 221	221 corkscrew
jīn tiān 901	901 today	kāi shǐ 88	88 begin
jǐn jí 941	941 urgent	kāide 633	633 open
jǐn shèn 172	172 caution	kàn jiàn 766	766 see
jìn 596	596 near	kǎo 734	734 roast
jīng cháng 28	28 always	kǎo shì 872	872 test
jīng yà 853	853 surprise	kē xué 756	756 science
jìng sài 213	213 competition	ké sòu 227	227 cough
jìngzi 568	568 mirror	kě 881	881 thirst
jiǔ 608	608 nine	kě kào 765	765 secure
jiǔ shí 610	610 ninety	kè rén 424	424 guest
jiǔ yuè 770	770 September	kōng 319	319 empty
jiù 629	629 old	kōng jiān 819	819 space
jiù yuán 724	724 rescue	kōng qì 19	19 air
júzi 635	635 orange	kǒng 454	454 hole
jù lí 277	277 distance	kǒudai 685	685 pocket
jùzi 753	753 saw	kòuzi 148	148 button

The Pinyin Transliteration

(alphabetized, according to pronunciation)

kǔ 241	cry	lǐ fà shī 430	hairdresser
kǔ 105	bitter	lǐ wù 402	gift
kùzi 921	trousers	lǐzi 684	plum
kuài 340	fast	lì shù 622	oak
kuàilè 682	pleasure	lì xī 477	interest
kūn chóng 475	insect	lián jià pǐn 66	bargain
lā jī 395	garbage	lián yī qún 291	dress
lā jī 964	waste	liǎn 335	face
là zhú 155	candle	liànzi 176	chain
lái 210	come	liǎo jiě 936	understand
lán 115	blue	lín jū 602	neighbor
lánzi 71	basket	lín yù 786	shower
lǎn duò 508	lazy	líng 1000	zero
lǎo shī 867	teacher	língzi 92	bell
lǎo shǔ 711	rat	lǐng dài 894	tie
léi shēng 890	thunder	liú 720	remain
lèi 900	tired	liù 796	six
lí hūn 280	divorce	liù shí 798	sixty
lí kāi 513	leave (to depart)	liù yuè 489	June
lízi 657	pear	lóng xiā 530	lobster

The Pinyin Transliteration

(alphabetized, according to pronunciation)

Pinyin	No.	English
lóngzi	252	deaf
lóu tī	826	staircase
lóu shàng	940	upstairs
lǘ	623	oar
lǘ sǔn	47	asparagus
lǘ	284	donkey
lǚ xíng	918	travel
lǜ sè	420	green
lǜ shī	507	lawyer
lún tāi	899	tire
luó sī	759	screw
máfan	920	trouble
mǎ	457	horse
mǎ péng	825	stable
mǎ yǐ	34	ant
mǎi	149	buy
mǎi mài	144	business
mài	768	sell
mǎn qī	331	expire
màn màn	804	slowly
māo	168	cat
máo jīn	910	towel
máo tǎn	109	blanket
máo zhī wù	989	wool
màozi	440	hat
méi	202	coal
měi lì	80	beautiful
mén	285	door
mèng	290	dream
mì fēng	84	bee
mì mì	764	secret
mián tù	225	cotton
mián bāo	129	bread
mián bāo shī fù	62	baker
miàn fěn	361	flour
miàn tiáo	613	noodle
míng tiān	905	tomorrow
míng xìn piàn	692	postcard
míngzi	594	name
mó shù	541	magic

The Pinyin Transliteration

(alphabetized, according to pronunciation)

mógu 588	mushroom	néng 1	able
mò shuǐ 474	ink	nǐ hǎoma? 463	how are you?
mǔ niú 232	cow	nián 995	year
mǔ zhǐ 889	thumb	nián qīng 999	young
mǔqin 578	mother	nián suì 16	age
mù dì 18	aim	niǎo 102	bird
mù shī 197	clergy	niǎo bù 266	diaper (baby's napkin)
mùtou 988	wood	niú nǎi 567	milk
ná 862	take	niú ròu 85	beef
nǎli? 977	where?	nóng mín 658	peasant
nàli 875	there	nǔ lì 311	effort
nǎi zhī 237	cream	nǚ ér 250	daughter
nán háizi 124	boy	nǚ háizi 403	girl
nán kàn 931	ugly	nǚ pú 542	maid
nán rén 547	man	nǚ xìng 345	female
nán xìng 545	male	nuǎn lú 843	stove
nánbian 818	south	nuǎnhuo 962	warm
nǎozi 126	brain	ōu qín 650	parsley
nǎo dùzi 267	diarrhea	pá 235	crawl
nèi yī 937	underwear	pà xiū 70	bashful

The Pinyin Transliteration

(alphabetized, according to pronunciation)

pánzi 276	dish	pū kè 679	playing card
páng guāng 107	bladder	pú táo jiǔ 984	wine
pǎo 741	run	pútao 416	grape
pǎo dào 742	runway	qī 772	seven
péi bàn 6	accompany	qī dài 328	expect
péi jià qián 288	dowry	qī shí 774	seventy
péng yǒu 383	friend	qī yuè 488	July
pí fū 799	skin	qí 184	chess
pí gé 512	leather	qí tā 636	other
pí jiǔ 86	beer	qǐ gài 87	beggar
pí wài yī 390	fur coat	qǐ lì 731	rise
piányi 180	cheap	qǐ zhòng jī 234	crane
piǎo bái 110	bleach	qì xī 132	breath
piào 892	ticket	qì yóu 399	gasoline (petrol)
píng 358	flat	qiān 509	lead
píng guǒ 38	apple	qiān 884	thousand
píng guǒ jiǔ 192	cider	qiān bǐ 660	pencil
píngzi 122	bottle	qiān míng 790	signature
pò bù 708	rag	qiān bāo 702	purse
pò huài 264	destroy	qiánzi 683	plier(s)

The Pinyin Transliteration

(alphabetized, according to pronunciation)

qiǎn zé 108	blame	rén zào 45	45 artificial
qiáng 846	strong	rěn nài 653	653 patience
qiáng 960	wall	rèn zhēn 771	771 serious
qiáo 135	bridge	róng yì 309	309 easy
qiē 246	cut	ròu 559	559 meat
qīng chǔ 196	clear	ròu diàn 145	145 butcher
qīng fù 157	capsize	ròu zhī 419	419 gravy
qǐng 681	please	rù diàn 554	554 mattress
qióng 688	poor	rù kǒu 321	321 entrance
qiū tiān 51	autumn	ruǎn 812	812 soft
qiú 64	ball	ruǎn xiàn 220	220 cord
qù 409	go	sāi 181	181 cheek
quán 373	fountain	sài mǎ 458	458 horserace
quán bù 22	all	sān 886	886 three
quán wēi 50	authority	sān shí 883	883 thirty
quántou 356	fist	sān yuè 550	550 March
quàn gào 10	advice	sǎnzi 932	932 umbrella
quē xí 3	absent	sàozhou 137	137 broom
qúnzi 800	skirt	sēn lín 369	369 forest
rè 460	hot	shāzi 750	750 sand

The Pinyin Transliteration

(alphabetized, according to pronunciation)

shā mò 262 desert
shā yú 776 shark
shān 579 mountain
shān yáng 410 goat
shǎn diàn 523 lightning
shāng diàn 841 store
shāng rén 564 merchant
shàng dì 411 God
shàng yóu 536 lubricating
shāo 118 boil
shāo 143 burn
shé 808 snake
shétou 906 tongue
shēn 256 deep
shēn tǐ 117 body
shèn zàng 491 kidney
shēng 712 raw
shēng mìng 519 life
shēng 955 voice
shēng qì 30 angry

shēng rì 104 birthday
shēng xiùde 743 rusty
shéngzi 738 rope
shèng dàn jié 190 Christmas
shī 975 wet
shīzi 526 lion
shīzi 534 louse
shí 870 ten
shí bā 314 eighteen
shí èr 927 twelve
shí èr yuè 255 December
shí jiān 895 time
shí jiān biǎo 896 timetable
shí jiǔ 609 nineteen
shí liù 797 sixteen
shí qī 773 seventeen
shí sān 882 thirteen
shí sì 375 fourteen
shí táng 271 dining room
shí wǔ 348 fifteen

shí wù 365	365 food	shǒu 434	434 hand
shí yī 318	318 eleven	shǒu dū 156	156 capital
shí yī yuè 617	617 November	shǒu jīn 435	435 handkerchief
shí yù 37	37 appetite	shǒu tào 407	407 glove
shí yuè 626	626 October	shǒu tí shì 690	690 portable
shítou 839	839 stone	shǒu zhǐ 352	352 finger
shí yòng 942	942 use	shǒu zhuó 125	125 bracelet
shì 75	75 be	shū 120	120 book
shì 923	923 try	shū cài 946	946 vegetable
shì 997	997 yes	shūhu 601	601 negligent
shì chǎng 551	551 market	shūzi 209	209 comb
shì gù 5	5 accident	shù 919	919 tree
shì jì 175	175 century	shù zì 619	619 number
shì jiàn 11	11 affair	shuāzi 140	140 brush
shì jiè 992	992 world	shuí? 979	979 who?
shì mín 194	194 citizen	shuǐ 966	966 water
shì zhǎng 557	557 mayor	shuǐ guǒ 387	387 fruit
shì zhèng tīng 912	912 town hall	shuǐ shǒu 747	747 sailor
shōu huò 439	439 harvest	shuì 866	866 tax
shōu jù 715	715 receipt	shuì jiào 803	803 sleep

The Pinyin Transliteration

(alphabetized, according to pronunciation)

Pinyin		English
shuō fú 664	664	persuade
sī chóu 791	791	silk
sī jī 294	294	driver
sǐ 253	253	death
sì 374	374	four
sì fēn zhī yī 703	703	quarter
sì shí 372	372	forty
sì yuè 41	41	April
sōng shù 673	673	pine tree
sòng 259	259	deliver
sòng 769	769	send
sù miáo 289	289	drawing
suān 817	817	sour
suàn 228	228	count
suàn zhàng 7	7	account
sǔn hài 247	247	damage
sǔn shī 533	533	loss
suǒ 531	531	lock
tā 443	443	he
tā 778	778	she
tài yáng 850	850	sun
tāng 816	816	soup
táng 848	848	sugar
táng xiōng dì 231	231	cousin
tīzi 498	498	ladder
tiān 251	251	day
tiān é róng 947	947	velvet
tiān kōng 801	801	sky
tiān qì 968	968	weather
tián 856	856	sweet
tiáo jiàn 214	214	condition
tiào rù 278	278	dive
tiào wàng 950	950	view
tiào zǎo 359	359	flea
tiě 480	480	iron
tīng 446	446	hear
tíng chē 649	649	parking
tíng zhǐ 840	840	stop
tóng 219	219	copper
tóng yì 17	17	agree

The Pinyin Transliteration

(alphabetized, according to pronunciation)

tǒng 68	68 barrel	wān lù 265	265 detour
tòng kǔ 640	640 pain	wán 678	678 play
tōu 833	833 steal	wán gù 847	847 stubborn
tóu 444	444 head	wán jù 913	913 toy
tóu 888	888 throw	wán ǒu 283	283 doll
tóu fà 429	429 hair	wǎn 123	123 bowl
tóu jīng 516	516 lens	wǎn 503	503 late
tóu míng 917	917 transparent	wǎn cān 272	272 dinner
tū 63	63 bald	wǎnshang 607	607 night
tú zhāng 828	828 stamp (seal)	wǎng 603	603 net (fishing)
tǔ dòu 695	695 potato	wàng jì 370	370 forget
tùzi 707	707 rabbit	wēi xiǎn 248	248 danger
tuǐ 515	515 leg	wēi xiǎn 732	732 risk
tūn 855	855 swallow	wéi fǎ 471	471 illegal
wāzi 384	384 frog	wéi fàn 953	953 violation
wáwa 54	54 baby	wéi jīn 754	754 scarf
wài 637	637 outside	wěiba 860	860 tail
wài guó 368	368 foreign	wèi 838	838 stomach
wài yī 203	203 coat	wèi hé zuìde 811	811 sober
wān dòu 655	655 pea	wèi shénme? 980	980 why?

The Pinyin Transliteration

(alphabetized, according to pronunciation)

wèidao	865	taste
wén	806	smell
wén jiàn	281	document
wénzi	577	mosquito
wèn	46	ask
wèn tí	704	question
wū dǐng	735	roof
wūzi	736	room
wǔ huā guǒ	350	fig
wú liáo	869	tedious
wǔ	357	five
wǔ fàn	538	lunch
wǔ shí	349	fifty
wǔ yuè	555	May
wù	364	log
xī	495	knee
xī	897	tin
xī shǔ	580	mouse
xībian	974	west
xí guàn	427	habit
xǐ	963	wash
xǐ yī diàn	505	laundry
xǐ zǎo	72	bath
xiā	111	blind
xià tiān	849	summer
xià wǔ	13	afternoon
xiàba	189	chin
xiānsheng	584	Mr (addressing)
xián bǐng	233	cracker
xiǎn shì	785	show
xiàn	428	hail
xiàn	885	thread
xiàn kuǎn	167	cash
xiàn zài	618	now
xiāng cháng	752	sausage
xiāng liào	821	spice
xiāng xìn	91	believe
xiǎng	880	think
xiǎngqi	721	remember
xiàng jiāo	740	rubber

The Pinyin Transliteration

(alphabetized, according to pronunciation)

xiàng hòu 57	57 backward		xīn 605	605 new
xiàng liàn 598	598 necklace		xīn niáng 134	134 bride
xiàng xià 287	287 down		xīn xiān 380	380 fresh
xiāo huà 270	270 digestion		xīn zàng 447	447 heart
xiāo shī 275	275 disappear		xìn 517	517 letter
xiāo xī 473	473 information		xìn fēng 322	322 envelope
xiǎo 805	805 small		xīng qī 971	971 week
xiǎo chuáng 238	238 crib		xīng qī èr 924	924 Tuesday
xiǎo dāozi 496	496 knife		xīng qī liù 751	751 Saturday
xiǎo fèi 898	898 tip		xīng qī sān 970	970 Wednesday
xiǎo hái 187	187 child		xīng qī sì 891	891 Thursday
xiǎo jiě 569	569 Miss (addressing)		xīng qī tiān 851	851 Sunday
xiǎo shí 461	461 hour		xīng qī wǔ 381	381 Friday
xiǎo tōu 877	877 thief		xīng qī yī 571	571 Monday
xiǎo xīn 161	161 careful		xīngxing 830	830 star
xiào 504	504 laugh		xíng lǐ 60	60 baggage
xiàohua 487	487 joke		xíng wéi 89	89 behavior
xié 782	782 shoe		xìng 40	40 apricot
xiě 993	993 write		xiōng pú 131	131 breast
xièxie 873	873 thanks		xiōng táng 185	185 chest

The Pinyin Transliteration
(alphabetized, according to pronunciation)

xióng 78	bear	
xǔ duō 586	much	
xǔ kě 662	permission	
xué xí 511	learn	
xué xiào 755	school	
xuě 809	snow	
xuě qiāo 802	sled	
xuě yú 205	codfish	
xuè 113	blood	
xún fú 864	tame	
xùn sù 705	quick	
yāzi 300	duck	
yá chǐ 908	tooth	
yá shuā 909	toothbrush	
yá yī 260	dentist	
yǎba 590	mute	
yà má bù 525	linen	
yān 296	drown	
yān 807	smoke	
yāntong 188	chimney	

yán 748	salt	
yán sè 208	color	
yǎn jīng 333	eye	
yǎn jìng 334	eyeglasses	
yǎn lèi 868	tears	
yàn mài 624	oats	
yáng 779	sheep	
yáng bái cài 150	cabbage	
yáng cōng 631	onion	
yáng gāo 500	lamb	
yàng pǐn 749	sample	
yāo dài 95	belt	
yào 560	medicine	
yào fáng 665	pharmacy	
yào pǐn 297	drug	
yàoshi 490	key	
yě 26	also	
yě xǔ 556	maybe	
yě yíng 154	camp	
yè 639	page	

The Pinyin Transliteration

(alphabetized, according to pronunciation)

Pinyin	No.	English		Pinyin	No.	English
yè tǐ	528	liquid		yīng táo	183	cherry
yèzi	510	leaf		yìng	438	hard
yī	630	one		yǒng qì	230	courage
yī fú	200	clothing		yóu	628	oil
yī lǐng	207	collar		yóu jiàn	543	mail
yī shēng	666	physician		yóu jú	693	post office
yī yuàn	459	hospital		yóu piào	827	stamp (mail)
yí bàn	431	half		yóu yǒng	857	swim
yí yuè	484	January		yóu zhá yú	382	fried fish
yíge	668	piece		yǒu	442	have
yǐ hòu	12	after		yǒu bìng	787	sick
yǐjīng	25	already		yǒu máo bìng	257	defective
yǐzi	177	chair		yǒu xiào	52	available
yì diǎn	347	few		yǒu zuì	426	guilty
yì qǐ	903	together		yòubian	728	right
yì shù	44	art		yòuzi	417	grapefruit
yì wù	302	duty		yú	355	fish
yīn wèi	81	because		yú kuài	680	pleasant
yín	792	silver		yǔ	709	rain
yìn shuā	698	printing		yǔ yán	501	language

The Pinyin Transliteration

(alphabetized, according to pronunciation)

yǔ yī 710	raincoat	
yù jiàn 561	meet	
yù mǐ 222	corn (maize)	
yù yī 73	bathrobe	
yuán 193	circle	
yuán 739	round	
yuǎn 338	far	
yuànzi 396	garden	
yuē dìng 39	appointment	
yuè 573	month	
yuèliang 574	moon	
yún cǎi 201	cloud	
yùn 481	ironing	
yùn chuán 761	seasick	
yùnqi 537	luck	
zá zhì 540	magazine	
zài 14	again	
zài hòu 90	behind	
zài jiàn 414	goodbye	
zài xià 94	below	
zài xià 934	under	
zàng 274	dirty	
zàng lǐ 389	funeral	
zǎo 304	early	
zǎo chén 576	morning	
zǎo fàn 130	breakfast	
zǎo pén 74	bathtub	
zào yīn 612	noise	
zēng hèn 441	hate	
zhǎi 595	narrow	
zhǎn lǎn huì 326	exhibition (display)	
zhàn 625	occupy	
zhàn 829	stand	
zhàn tái 677	platform	
zhàn zhēng 961	war	
zhāngláng 204	cockroach	
zhàng dān 101	bill	
zhàngfu 468	husband	
zhàngpeng 871	tent	
zhè lǐ 451	here	

The Pinyin Transliteration

(alphabetized, according to pronunciation)

zhēn 401 genuine
zhēn 600 needle
zhēn shí 922 truth
zhěntou 671 pillow
zhèn 911 town
zhèng miàn 386 front
zhèng què 223 correct
zhèng rén 986 witness
zhī fáng 341 fat
. . . zhī jiān 99 between
zhǐ 844 straight
zhí wù 676 plant
zhí yè 700 profession
zhǐ 632 only
zhǐ 645 paper
zhǐ bǎn 160 cardboard
zhǐ jiǎ 353 fingernail
zhì dòng qì 127 brake
zhōng jiān 566 middle
zhōng wǔ 614 noon

zhòng 448 443 heavy
zhòng liàng 972 972 weight
zhǒu 316 316 elbow
zhū 669 669 pig
zhū ròu 689 689 pork
zhuā zhù 169 169 catch
zhuān 133 133 brick
zhuǎn 926 926 turn
zhuōzi 859 859 table
zǐ 767 767 seed
zǐ dàn 142 142 bullet
zì xíng chē 100 100 bicycle
zì yóu 379 379 free
zǒu 959 959 walk
zuǐ 581 581 mouth
zuǐ chún 527 527 lip
zuó tiān 998 998 yesterday
zuǒbian 514 514 left
zuò 544 544 make
zuò 795 795 sit

A List of the Original Complex Characters

Although this Basic Words Dictionary follows the modern development of the Chinese language in the direction of stroke simplification, the following list gives the full form for all the words, since the classical (also called "complicated" or "traditional") characters are still in wide use, especially outside the area of the People's Republic.

1画
一 630
一月 484
一半 431
一個 668
一起 797
一點 903
一點 347

2画
三 929
三十 928
三月 344
七 772
七月 774
七十 488
八 313
八十 315
八月 48
九 608
九十 610
九月 770
下午 870
十一 318

十二 927
十三 882
十四 375
十五 348
十六 797
十七 773
十八 314
十九 609
十月 626
十一月 617
十二月 255
丁字花 524
人造 45
入口 321
…之間 99

3画
三 886
三十 883
三月 550
下午 13
下巴 189

上羊 410
上油 536
上帝 411
丈夫 468
也 26
也許 556
乞丐 87
叉子 371
千 884
工作 991
工具 907
工資 956
工廠 336
土豆 695
大 502
大理石 549
牧羊 67
大好 883
大姊 397
大腿 878
小 805

小刀子 496
小心 161
小床 238
小組 569
小後 187
小時 461
小愉 877
小費 898
口袋 685
山 579
已經 25
子彈 142
女性 345
女兒 250
女佣子 403
女僕 542
天 251

4画
天空 801
天氣 968
天鵝絨 947

夫人 585
五 357
五十 349
五月 555
六 796
六十 798
六月 489
不 611
不同 269
牙刷 909
牙齒 908
牙醫 260
互相 591
中午 614
中間 566
午飯 538
以後 12
內衣 937
公牛 638
公寓 35

About the Author

PETER M. BERGMAN is a scholar and a linguist. He is the president and publisher of Polyglot Library. He also compiled the <u>Concise Dictionary of 26 Languages</u>, available in a Signet edition.